Dragoons

C Troop 1/1 Armored Cavalry, Vietnam 1967-1972

By

Grant Coble

authorHOUSE

1663 Liberty Drive, Suite 200
Bloomington, Indiana 47403
(800) 839-8640
www.AuthorHouse.com

© 2005 Grant Coble. All Rights Reserved.

No part of this book may be reproduced, stored in a retrieval system, or transmitted by any means without the written permission of the author.

First published by AuthorHouse 01/13/05

ISBN: 1-4208-1281-5 (sc)

Printed in the United States of America
Bloomington, Indiana

This book is printed on acid-free paper.

Introduction

The stories you are about to read are the memories of Troopers from Charlie Troop, 1st Squadron, 1st Regiment of Dragoons. The time span covers the years from 1967 to 1972 in which the 1/1 was stationed in Republic of South Vietnam, in Indochina.

Each story is as the story teller saw the event unfold and remembers after some 30 plus years. While more than one person may tell of the same event, no two are the same as each tells his version and each is actual. In a combat Armored unit, each crew member is busy during a firefight, emergency, or even during a time when all is quiet and well, will see an event unfold with his own set of eyes and what others on his crew may not see. This, in itself, is why a crew must always work as one, keeping the other crew members abreast of important events surrounding him as the other crew members may be involved with a different set of problems.

You will read the names of our fallen comrades, how they died, the date, their home town, and the location on the 'Wall' in Washington, DC, of which they've been immortalized. Also, who the Troop Commanders were at the time and were located during the 5 year span. When official records could be found pertaining to C Troop, they were also added. Stories of humor, sadness, fear, terror, and just plain everyday life will help you understand the life a Trooper lived during his time in Vietnam.

While one who has never experienced combat will ever understand what goes through the minds of those who have, before, during, and after; you can at least read and learn how they lived their everyday lives, and maybe, just maybe, develop a better understanding of who they are and why.

The gut twisting fear before going into a battle you know will happen. Your military trained mind kicks in as you react to each moment during a battle, without thinking about your action, knowing that if you do stop to think about the moment, you will die.

The period after a fight when you thank God your still alive, yet sit numb, stunned, and shaking; wondering only then how you accomplished some of the "Beyond" human feats of endurance and strength that helped you survive.

Only then to have fear set in, the shakes, the pain, sadness, and the guilty feeling you are still alive and yet wonder why when your fellow comrade died. The long, hollow, empty blank stare a combat soldier develops.

The lasting memories that never go away, but get buried in the back of your mind, and praying everyday it won't surface this day. Of simple sounds common and unnoticed by the general public, yet to the veteran capable of gushing to the surface the memories you so desperately want to stay buried.

You will read stories by individuals suffering still from the War. The everlasting guilt felt by each. Could they have done more; seen something to warn them; been at a different location; not missed an enemy soldier; seen a ambush coming; tracked correctly; not break down.

The fact is we are human, subject to mistakes, missing the obvious, talking, eating, or what ever the reason may have been. And as humans, subject to all the emotions inherited by us.

Within that invisible shield every combat soldier wears, is a person wearing very deep scars, carefully concealed. Scars he wishes to protect himself from as well as those around him.

Not all scars are visible to the naked eye. The mental scars of the Combat Veteran run deep and for some inflict great pain. A pain that never goes away nor treatable with medication. For some, a life of drinking alcohol; for others; drug abuse; some turn to religion; while a few, desperate and beyond help, racked by pain, enter or are committed to a medical institution, or take their lives. You will get to peep into individuals lives and what they still live with daily.

One often hears the phrase, "War is Hell." But, so is life for some after. Things happen in war beyond the control of the GI. Innocent civilians get caught in the cross fire of combat with deadly results. War does not segregate by age. Lives, homes, futures, and history are destroyed and changed by war. Accidents do happen and individuals must live with that the best way they can. Atrocities against mankind are uncommon, yet well published. The vast majority of American units in South Vietnam greatly frowned on such behavior as did the individuals attached to those units.

The names you read are actual. These men lived and, and in some cases died, that you, an American, can have the freedom to worship as you chose, freedom of speech, to vote, travel, or work where you want. To have freedom of choice. Freedom of political choice with out fear of persecution. One nation, one Flag; a nation's people comprised of a great variety of national, ethnic, and social background living under one Flag. Many Americans have died before us, and sadly, many will die after us.

While in the rear, or secured base camps, there were incidents between soldiers. Yet, put in the field together, they became one; inseparable, comrades, and some of the toughest, meanest fighting men one could ever hope to serve with.

We invite you to sit back and read about our life experiences during our tour in Vietnam. The sequence of events have been put in order by date of event to help you follow the 5 years during the unit's stay. While most of what has been told is non-graphic, there are some parts of stories that are. Profanity will be found and was used, mostly, in describing an action packed moment during battle.

Credits

Story Collection By
Grant Coble

Editor
Joann Coble

Story Contributions:
John Ahrenberg
Steve Bolton
Paul Caven
Grant Coble
Mike Collicchio
James Dean
Randall Densmore
Ron Dougherty
Pete Harrington
David Hill
Joel Alvin Jefferson
James Kronner
David Miller
Thomas Motley
David Pitmon
Carl Wronko
Ken Yarborough

Poem Contributions
Anthony John Newman
Robert Hillman
Scott "Tex" Gideon

Historical Data:
John LaRoche
Steve Bolton

Research Contributions
Stephen Maxner, Associate Director, Archivist, The Vietnam Archive, Texas Tech University

This book is dedicated to our fallen comrades who paid the ultimate price that others may live and be free. May their names never be lost or forgotten by time or man.

Charlie Troop, 1st Squadron, 1st Regiment of Dragoons, killed in action in the Republic of South Vietnam, 1967 to 1972.

Charles Henry Adams, Bruce Lyle Badger, Richard Charles Balukonis, John Dabney Bass, Edgar L Bolding, Terry Lee Bosworth, Perry Leonard Bozemen, Gerald Jacob Budbill, Stephen Walter Burgdorfer, Sheldon John Burnett, Horace Lee Burton, Kenneth Allan Butler Jr., Thomas Butler, James Anthony Cabral Jr, Joseph Carlos Carvajal, Charles Don Champion, Eugene Paul Clark, Robert C Coonrad, George Herman Coppage III, Joe Edward Crenshaw, Dominick Lawrence Cuccia, Stephen William Cummings, Alan Eunice Davis, Donald Gary Dillard, Micheal William Elden, Mario Pereda Estrada, Jere Douglas Farnow, Charles Grady Floyd, Gary Freeman, Edelmiro Leonel Garcia Sr., Kenneth Mervin Gray, Willie Edward Glover, David Eugene Gossard, Lawrence Day Greef, Marion Tracy Griffin, Dale Andre Gronsky, David Oscar Haake, Marloye Keith Halgrimson, Allan Dewey Hanlan, Maurice J Hass, Harold Henasey, William James Hillard II, Coleman Gee Hillman, Kimmey Dean Hobbs, Martin Reinholdt Huart Jr, Larry Anthony Jackson, Philop Robert Jamrock, James Larry Johnson, Randy Truman Kendle, George John Kohlmeir III, Jimmy Kuhlenhoelter, Thomas Lee Lafferty, Howard Sidney Lamb, Stephen M Lashinsky Jr, Larry Leamon, James Linder Jr, Jack Ray Lockridge, Neal Lord, Joe Love Jr, Quillard Frank Lyons, Carmine Angelo Macedonio, Charles Deo Maloney, Raymond Raliford Mays, William McMurtrey, Micheal Dwaine Newland, Steve Owen Nussbaumer, Raymond Joseph Palandro, James Willard Powers Jr, Donald Pyrand, Robert Herman Rassel, Richard Alvin Renfro, Cordell Bruce Rogers, Richard Lee Rowland Jr., Michael Jorn Saunders, Richard E Saldana, James Ellison Scott, William Sharpe Jr., Paul Wayne Shrewsbury, Bradley Joseph Simmons, Claudias Augustus Small, Edsel Wayne Steagall, Edward Samuel Stewart, Larry Strahan, Lawrence Marvin Svobodny, William Alan Swoveland, Arlie Terry, Homer Daniel Thick, Tomas Valerio, Elisio Vergara, David Lorenzo Vigil, Manasseh Brock

Warren, Henry Braxton Williams, Hillard Evans Williams, Richard Frank Williams, Otto Tom Weben, Ronald J Wojtkiewics

    I stand before you, my brothers, at attention, and salute with great pride to have known you, and great sorrow to have lost you. God bless you my brothers, Amen.

Table of Contents

Introduction v
Credits ix
1967 1
1968 33
1969 65
1970 93
1971 159
1972 191

1967

The stories you are about to read are true as seen and remembered by members of a combat unit during the years of 1967 through 1972, in a place few wished to be, called Vietnam, located in South East Asia. The unit, Charlie Troop 1 Squadron, 1 Regiment of Dragoons- an armored cavalry unit, was located primarily at a base called Chu Lia, about 50 miles south of Da Nang. Charlie Troop was part of a Squadron that consisted of 3 Troops and a Headquarters unit. Each unit consisted of 3 platoons with 7 APC's (Armored Personal Carriers) and 3 tanks (M-48 and M-60's, and after 1969-Sheridans), manned by 4 men each. Support personal included mechanics, cooks, and clerks.

Chu Lai was bordered by mountains on one side and the clear, blue, China Sea with its white sandy beaches on the other The location was critical in stopping supplies for the Vietcong and NVA (North Vietnamese Army) south bound. While this may not have stopped the flow, it slowed the supplies needed by the communist aggressors.

The war, as known by the American combat soldier and the American public, was not a declared war, and was only considered a police action. The soldier's social background ranged from college educated to high school dropout. From volunteer to draftee, from wanting to go to Vietnam to avoiding prison and forced to join the military. Fathers, uncles, sons, brothers- all with a common purpose, to serve and survive. What they had in common was a brotherly love forged by combat, duty, and the desire to live. What you got was C Troop, the "Mean Green Fighting Machine."

The country was inhabited primarily by farmers, with villages, towns and cities mostly located along or near the ocean. The farmers were a simple people with simple life styles - or at least during the day. Many (old and young, women and children), at night, became know as VC, or Viet Cong. Planning attacks on Americans and their Allies, ambushing, planting mines, out right attacks, sniping, spying, and what ever else they could do to disrupt the pacification ideas America had in mind was their mission.

American soldiers never lost a battle during the 11 years in Vietnam. In 1975 Vietnam fell to North Vietnam and at last became one country. This was Ho Chi Min's dream of which he did not live to see.

The names of soldiers, places, and events are actual. The stories are as seen and written by members of C Troop. As some 30 years have passed, our memories have faded some so therefore, it is possible that two or more stories you read may be of the same event with a different twist. In the event the use of an actual name may lead to possible repercussions by any unnamed agency, organization, individual, or not wished to be used by the writer, no name will be used.

Campaigns conducted by Charlie Troop, 1/1 Cavalry during the Vietnam War:

Counteroffensive, Phase III
Tet Counteroffensive
Counteroffensive, Phase IV
Counteroffensive, Phase V
Counteroffensive, Phase VI
Tet 69/Counteroffensive
Summer-Fall 1969
Winter-Spring 1970
Sanctuary Counteroffensive
Consolidation I
Consolidation II
Cease-Fire

Decoration Streamers

Presidential Unit Citation (Army), Streamer embroidered, Tam Ky, Hoi An

Valorous Unit Award, Streamer embroidered, Quan Tin Province

Valorous Unit Award, Streamer embroidered, Quang Tin, Quang Ngai

Vietnamese Cross of Gallantry with Palm, Streamer embroidered, 1967-1970

Vietnamese Cross of Gallantry with Palm, Streamer embroidered, 1971

Vietnamese Cross of Gallantry with Palm, Streamer embroidered, 1967-1972

Presidential Unit Citation For Action In Vietnam Reads:

The Presidential Unit Citation (Army) For Extraordinary Heroism To The 1st Squadron, 1st Cavalry
And
Troop C, 7th Squadron, 17th Cavalry, United States Army

The 1st Squadron, 1st Cavalry and Troop C, 7th Squadron, 17th Cavalry, Americal Division, distinguished themselves by extraordinary heroism while engaged in military operations against hostile forces in that Republic of Vietnam from 31 January to 31 March 1968. During this period, these units encountered heavily armed, well supplied, and aggressive North Vietnamese and Viet Cong forces of company, battalion, and regimental size in more than 217 separate engagements in the southern I Corps tactical area in the vicinity of Tam Ky and Hoi An. Opposing a highly motivated enemy that consistently occupied heavily fortified bunkers and tunnel complexes with excellent fields of fire, the 1st Squadron, 1st Cavalry, supported by Troop C, 7th Squadron, 17th Cavalry, employed rapid movement, tenacious pursuit, and violent assault to defeat the enemy, killing 1,046 North Vietnamese and Viet Cong while sustaining only 11 fatal casualties of their own. Through their magnificent efforts, the 1st Squadron, 1st Cavalry and Troop C, 7th Squadron, 17th Cavalry added materially to the successes attained by the Americal Division on the field of battle. The conspicuous gallantry and extraordinary heroism displayed by all members of both units are in keeping with the highest traditions of military service and reflect great credit on them, the Americal Division, and the United States Army.

Note: All troopers are authorized to wear the Presidential Unit Citation while a member of the 1st Squadron, 1st Cavalry.

Valorous Unit Awards, Republic Of Vietnam

The citation reads as follows:

The 1st Squadron, 1st Cavalry (First Regiment of Dragoons) an its attached unit, F Troop, 8th Cavalry, distinguished themselves by extraordinary heroism while engaged in military operations in the Republic of Vietnam during the period 24 August through 25 September 1968. On three separate occasions during this period, the cavalrymen encountered heavily armed, well-entrenched, and determined Viet Cong and North Vietnamese Army units operation in their area of responsibility. Employing sound planning, bold and aggressive leadership, and dynamic and forceful execution, the men of the 1st Squadron, 1st Cavalry (First Regiment of Dragoons) repeatedly defeated their adversary and completed all assigned missions in an exemplary manner. Despite the rigors and hardships of the combat environment, unit personnel retained the high level of morale and esprit di corps which enabled them to prevail over an unrelenting and often numerically superior foe. With pride and dedication, the members of the squadron have materially advanced the Free World military effort in the Republic of Vietnam. The extraordinary heroism and devotion to duty displayed by the men of the 1st Squadron, 1st Cavalry(First Regiment of Dragoons) are in keeping with the highest traditions of the military service and reflect distinct credit upon themselves, their unit, and the Armed Forces of the United States.

> **Note: The 1st Squadron was later awarded a second Valorous Unit Award for action in Vietnam. All members of the 1st Squadron, 1st Cavalry are authorized to wear the Valorous Unit Award with Oak Leaf Cluster while a member of the organization.**

1967-1968, LTC Rich Harrington, Squadron Commander

1/1967 to 1/1968, Ralph P. Brown, Captain, Troop Commander, Captain Brown brought Charlie Troop over to South Vietnam from Fort Hood, Texas.

3/1967, Thomas "Action" Motley (My nick name is Action, a name given to me by my second track commander, Jerry Quesenberry. I was in the 1st platoon and served from March of 1967 to March 20th of 1968 (I was a Spec. E4). I arrived with Harold Stephens, nickname Whitey, Robert Miller, and Michael Saunders from the

1/52 Infantry. We had finished our Advanced Infantry Training. We were the best shots with the M-60 which qualified us for the Cav. I was Millers and Saunders acting Squad Leader and knew them very well. I met Stephens when we arrived and we became good friends. We were assigned to the 1st Platoon upon arrival. Miller and Saunders were assigned to C-10 and Stephens and I to C-12. He was 5 foot tall, 99 pounds soaking wet, and blond. Later we gave him the nick name Whitey. Also assigned to C-12 was Staff Sergeant Vernom, Spec. 4 Scharage, and later Spec. 4 Koller - just before shipping out. Because Koller was a Spec 4 and I a PFC, he took my position on the M-60. I became the M-79 Man with my trusty 45 caliber pistol at side. I was really pissed off with this move.

    We flew to California where our Squadron boarded the troop carrier The Johnny Walker for a 18 day cruise to Vietnam. We pulled guard at night at various locations on the ship along with "Head" duty (bathroom) and KP (mess hall) during the day. We played cards, board games, and watched movies at a make shift theater on deck. A lot of the guys would blow up their air mattress at night for the movie, taking up a lot of the sitting space. This did not go down to well so us smokers would throw our butts on the rolling deck and wait for a mattress to deflate, pissing the owner off. For other entertainment we would stand on deck and watch for whales or jelly fish.

    One day a storm hit and Whitey and I went to the bow of the ship to ride the waves. The Captain of the Ship saw us and ordered us to the Bridge on his loud speaker. He asked us if we were trying to get ourselves killed and we replied, "Hell, we're going to Vietnam and what are our chances of getting killed there?"

    Our sleeping quarters, 3 decks below were hot and stale. I was in the top bunk of 3 with steam and water pipes just overhead. The only way I could get into the bunk was for 2 guys to pick me up in a prone position and slide me in. That's how tight it was. Below us was the cargo hold filled with ammo crates. "Sure was glad the VC and NVA didn't have Submarines to blow us out of the water!"

    The 16th day we arrived at Okinawa and were given a 24 hour pass. We drank 4 saloons dry and started on our 5th when we noticed Patterson missing. Patterson was always getting into trouble with the women so Whitey and I went looking for him. One of the guys said he saw him leave with a girls so at 1AM in the morning we went looking for him in the valley. At one point some of the local men came at us with clubs and knives so we departed the area and headed back to the bar. As we walked in, out from the back door came Patterson with a girl on his neck and dress over his head.

Whitey and I went back to the ship and watched for the next 2 hours as our brothers returned. It looked like the crew from the movie, Mr Robertson. Not one person was sober. They came back by truck, jeep, bus, bike, motorcycle, or MP guard. A few fell into the water and had to be fished out.

9/1967, Unit arrived in I Corp Tactical Zone, South Vietnam

We arrived in Vietnam in late August off the coast of Da Nang. We boarded landing craft which took us ashore. As we approached shore we watched Gun Ships strafing the trees. Asking a sailor if that wasn't close. His reply was "There are no front lines in Vietnam". We landed, loaded into some trucks, and left for Chu Lai to fit our equipment for combat.

9/1967, The commanding General wanted us to guard the air base but our Commander disagreed so from that point we were in "Indian Country". This is what we trained for.

We spent the next 2 weeks waiting for our orders and pulling guard duty.

One night about 2AM Whitey and I heard some noise from the hill while pulling guard in a bunker. It sounded like someone digging and we called 6 (the Captain) for permission to fire the M-60 but were refused. "Can we shoot off flares?" With the ok we shot some flares off and the digging sound would stop each time. I figured sure the VC were digging a tunnel into our base. The next day some infantry guys went out but found nothing.

That night our platoon was ordered out on a night patrol with tanks and APC's. One of the tanks got stuck in a paddy and we broke 6 of our 8 cables trying to pull it. We spent the rest of the night waiting for a tank retriever to come and pull us out.

Whitey and I were on guard duty. We could hear some noises that sounded like the whole NVA army was coming after us. We were on pins and needles all night. About a ¼ mile away a fire fight broke out. You could see red and green tracers all over the place. This lasted about ½ hour. Later found out some grunts had set up an ambush and some VC came through.

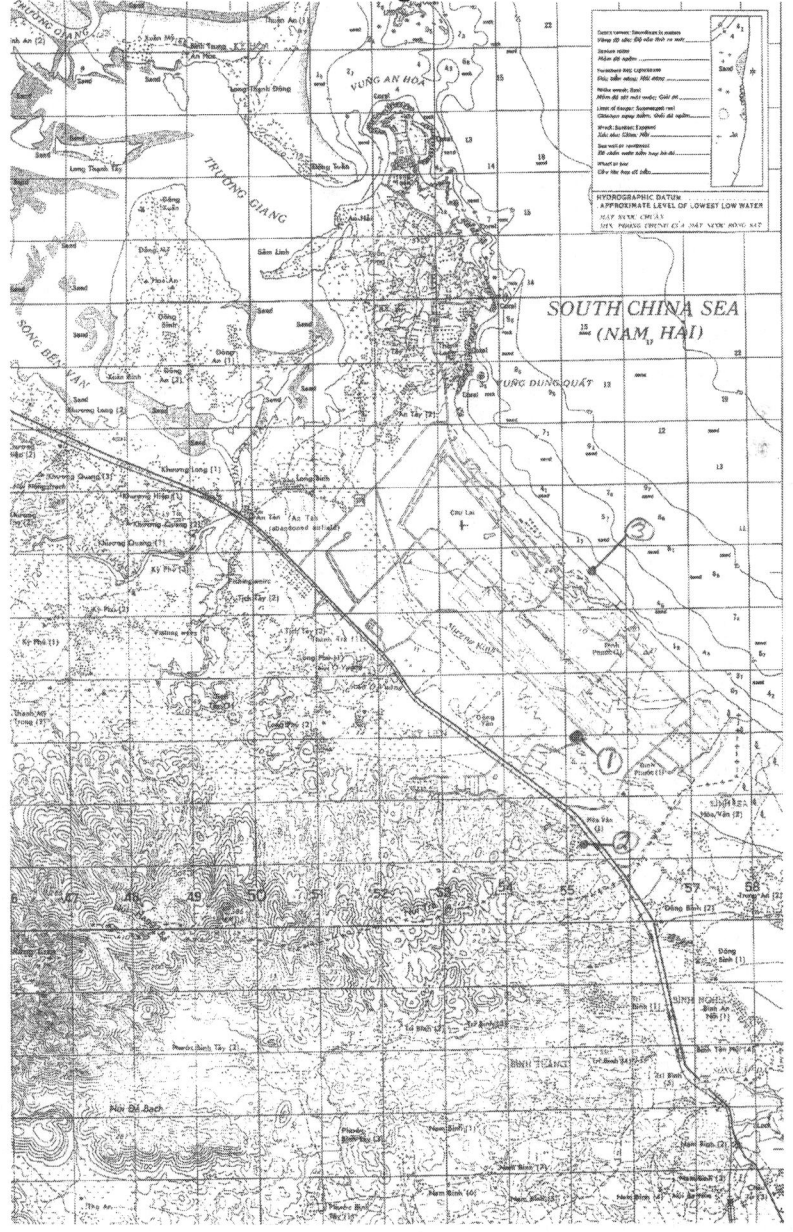

This map is of the Chu Lai AO. Noted locations are noted by number; 1. C Troop's base camp, 2. LZ Bayonet, 3. South China Sea beach. Down town Chu Lai was located at the far northern end of the air base. The long lines parallel to the base are the French Railway and Highway 1.

Anthony John Newman, "Reason,"
Sitting on a track,
In the middle of the night.
Watching for an attack,
So scared that they might.

Incoming! Incoming! Goes up the cry,
Green and red tracers light up the sky.
The anger of machine guns can be heard all around,
Screams an cries of partners hitting the ground.

To stop the Red Peril?
For Mom and apple pie?
To defend "Old glory?"
For this we might die?

  As the sun came up we could see what the noise was - water running down 3 layers of broken dikes. The tank retriever showed up and some guys jumped into the water. It was 3 foot deep. The tank retriever pulled the tank out and when the guys came out of the water, they found themselves covered with leeches. We burned off the leeches, loaded up and returned to camp.

  The next day we pulled out and went to a small hill called 34, I think, located about 40 miles from Chu Lai. The main gate to our camp was located in the center of town and the back gate at the north end of town. As we pulled into the camp many young girls came to greet us saying "GI Boom Boom!" I turned to SGT Vernom asking what that meant? He said I'd find out sooner or later. "Boy did I!"

  After setting up camp we stored some of our gear in some wooden buildings, which was the last our platoon would have for the duration of our tour.

The CO, Captain Brown, called us together and said he was going to send the medics into the village and check out the girls for any diseases and mark the ones infected. He didn't mind us having some fun, just didn't want any one catching anything. "You can go into the village from 7 to 11am and have all the fun you want". You never saw a happier bunch of guys! I was hoping our whole tour would be spent here. The next morning off we went and by 11 we all had a girl friend. I figured Whitey being as good looking as he was would get the best looking girl and "Boy" was I wrong. He introduced me to her the next day and she was stone ugly. I asked him "Why" and his reply was "Some staff sergeant dumped her and broke her heart". I felt sorry for him.

My girls name was To Lee and very good looking. She wasn't one of the local whores. We had many good conversations together. I met her mother and father and her mother became my laundry girl. I bought my beer from her. Their house was located in front of the motor pool and whenever there To Lee would bring ice cold beers.

The village was off limits to us at night. Lt. Mantua would take some guys and patrol the village at night to make sure we stayed clear. The word was the VC would do R&R at night while we did R&R during the day.

One night 3 tanks were pulling guard at the main gate. There was a hutch about 20 foot in front of the gate with many girls staying there. They wanted to party this night and we figured as long as we were not on guard, why not. We invited them in but they wanted us to come to their place instead. Once I was relieved from guard duty, I joined the party. Whitey came in late. We sat around joking and laughing when we heard "Halt, who goes there!" It got quiet real quick. "Lt Mantua and the village patrol!" "Oh Shit" was said in a soft voice. One of the girls asked what was wrong and we told her that if caught here we'd be in a world of hurt. "Come with me, I'll hide you." She led us to a small hutch, opened the door, and in we went. I could smell something rank and asked Patterson if he shit his pants. He wondered the same about me. About that time we heard a "Oink" and realized we were laying in a pig pen full of shit. Mantua left and we quickly got back to our tracks. The guys asked what the hell we fell into. "Don't ask," was our reply.

Next morning Lt. Mantua pulled us all together and proceeded to chew our ass. "Were it not for so many of you I'd give you an Article 15." Then he really got into my shit. Guess he figured I was the most responsible one and knew better. I explained we were all close by in case of trouble. "That's beside the point, it was wrong,", he said.

The next day, 1st Platoon moved out for a search and recon mission about 5 miles South East, near the China Sea. A destroyer was on station to offer us support should we need it. You could see her laying just off shore. We dismounted, leaving 2 guys on each track and went out into the paddies. Over the trees came a crop duster at about 150 feet spraying something over us. We had heard the government was spraying something to defoliate Charlies cover. I quickly put on my gas mask which I always carried. SGT Vernom ordered me to take the mask off.

"No one else had one and I was not to use mine," he said.

I replied, "That's their problem."

His response was, "Makes no difference,"

I held my breath as long as I could and kept my eyes closed until the spray was gone. Shortly after the plane left the LT. ordered us back as the mission was cancelled. I felt we were set up as guinea pigs for a government experiment.

Once we got back I took off all my cloths, showered twice, and took the cloths to Ma Ma Son and had her wash them twice to ensure all the chemicals were out.

A few days later Lt Mantua informed us we would be making "Thunder Runs" up and down Highway 1 during the night. This was to discourage the VC from setting up ambushes and planting mines. We wondered what General thought up this idea. 1st Platoon scout section would go north and 2nd south for 40 miles each. We took turns with C-10 and C-11 first and then C-12 and C-13 (each APC has a number. The letter signifies the Troop. The first number- the platoon, and the second number-the track) It was real scary traveling at night with your head lights on. I sat just behind the driver. Lucky for us the only action seen were Black Hawks with wing spans of 3 foot wide. Our head lights seemed to draw them and we hit a few with the splash board. We sped along at 45 mph until we reached the bridge guarded by the Arvin's. Whitey would hit the left turn lever real hard, spinning the track around, kicking up dirt and stones, scaring the hell out of the soldiers. This lasted about 2 weeks before we stopped.

During our stay at the camp, Whitey and I came up with a better way to stack our ammo. You stand on the ammo cans and when firing the 60's and as the cans get empty you begin to lose a good foot hold as the cans are removed. The two layers did make for good mine protection. We took the benches out and made ammo racks. We found we could stack 4 across and 7 high, giving us 28 cans each plus another 400 rounds in the shield giving us another 6000 rounds for the M-60. We also made a rack on the floor for the 50 cal giving it some 5000 rounds plus one case of hand grenades, 2 laws, 20,000 rounds of M-16, 5000 rounds of 45 cal, and a case of C-4. We also carried 100 rounds for the M-79. This gave us a lot of fire power. It also worked better for us during a fire fight as we could reach the ammo with out taking our eyes off the enemy. Soon the other tracks adopted this idea. You guys who came later have Whitey and I to thank for it.

9/13/1967, Michael Colicchio, 2nd Platoon was assigned to Task Force Oregon and was in convoy on a minor road leading to a village west of the city of Tam Ky, in the Quang Tim Province of the Republic of Vietnam. At that time, the Armored Personnel Carrier (APC), C-26, driven by PFC Lawrence Svobodny detonated an anti-tank mine, killing PFC Svobondny. I was the Rear Observer on the APC, C-20, immediately ahead of C-26 in the convoy, facing C-26. One of my responsibilities was to ensure that the track behind mine was "tracking" us; riding with its tracks/treads in the tracks of the vehicle in front of him, thereby minimizing the possibility of detonating a mine. Usually, Larry was attentive to my direction and followed my signals correcting his location. On this occasion, I could not get his attention; he was on the intercom with our platoon leader, Lt. Rhesa Barksdale (C-26), and was engaged in conversation, over his shoulder, with our Platoon medic; not paying attention to the road or me. Frustrated, I shook my head and thought, and I remember this vividly, "I hope he hits a small mine to wake him up." I looked down and within seconds, I heard an explosion, and when I looked up, the engine compartment cover was approximately 50 feet in the air. The explosion flipped the C-26 vehicle, severing Svobodny's foot and killing him. SPC-4 Greg Weislogel, of Erie Pennsylvania, was injured in the incident, receiving a Purple Heart.

9/13/1967, Lawrence Marvin Svobodny, Mahnomen, MN, Landmine, 26E/68

Anthony John Newman, "Virgin Warrior,"
Too young to drink,
Too young to vote,
Too young to fuck,
Too young to smoke.

Too young to handle with such ease,
These lethal actions, a general to please.
Too young to kill and maim for glory,
Too young, by far, to live this story.

Too young, by much, to live a lie,
And far too young, for this, to die.

9/1967, Thomas Motley, We were ordered to Thunder Road, about 50 miles south of Chu Lia. The name came from all the mines planted there. The new camp was on top of a 1000 foot mountain over looking the sea. We replaced a company of infantry who went on a month long mission in the central highlands. The one area our vehicles could not go. We arrived about 9AM and had a mine sweeper lead the way up. Once on top, we split up and took up defensive positions. 2nd Platoon had the north side overlooking the water while we had the southwest side overlooking a valley. Our missions consisted of road guards, mine sweeps, day and night missions, and ambushes.

The ambushes were voluntary and after 12 we could get a Combat Infantry Badge (CIB). About 75% volunteered for this duty. Whitey, Miller, Saunder and myself did so because we had training in the infantry and knew what to do. This was the start of the monsoon season and we were never dry. Sometimes it rained so hard you could not see for 5 feet in front of you at night. This made it real scary.

One night while on guard I went to several bunkers and retrieved some M-79 rounds. I collected a dozen for myself of which one was a canister round. When on patrol, SGT Vernom would have me pull rear guard. He figured that with the canister round I could blow anyone away plus warn the others at the same time. You could hear the steel balls rolling around in the round. We never ran into any trouble during the first 12 ambushes. I always had that canister round chambered. Lucky for us as later I found out that round was a dud.

I always carried 36 rounds of M-79, 2 belts of M-60, 8 clips of 45 cal, 4 hand grenades, and 1 clay more mine. Whitey asked me why I carried so much and I replied, "To fight our way out or until help arrived."

9/18/1967, One night SGT Brook took his men out to their ambush site. One of the guys had to take a shit which held them up for about 20 minutes. Lucky for them because 10 minutes before they reached the ambush site mortars and machine gun fire opened up on it. Brook's called Lt. Brown and told him what was happening. The LT ordered us to mount up and save them. We drove out to the location with our head lights off so not to give away our position. We arrived onto a hill overlooking the valley that SGT Brook was in. We could see the mortars hitting and the machine gun fire. Lt. Mantua ordered Whitey and me to dismount without flashlights and find a way down the hill. You couldn't see 10 feet in front of you. We tripped over rocks, fell into holes, and came to 8 foot cliff. The LT ordered us back.

As we approached the tracks we noticed red and green flickers going over the tracks, The VC were now firing at the noise of our tracks. We mounted up and with our track in the lead, we drove like mad men, everyone holding on for dear lives down the hill. It was like riding a wild bronco horse. When we reached the bottom of the hill we found SGT Brook's and his men. Charlie was beginning to zero in on us so everyone loaded up and we got the hell out of there.

We called for fire support and the Major came in with 2 gun ships and began firing at the flashes of gun fire. No one was hurt. SGT Vernom was mad because no one said thank you for saving them.

After getting back we figured someone was a spy. Who would know when and where we would set up an ambush? We decided our Vietnamese Scout was the spy and turned him over to the local authorities. It turned out later he was. SGT Brook became our interpreter. He came to us from Special Forces.

The following morning our cook was killed by a booby trap in his oven. We got rid of our local help and from that time on no locals were allowed in our camp. We were given orders to shoot anyone that tried to come in.

9/20/1967, David Eugene Gossard, Cook, Lima, OH, Multiple Fragmentation Wounds, 26E/96

Two days later a local man came to our tracks while on road duty and told us VC were in the village. We called 16 and informed him what was said. He said to wait until the rest of the platoon could join up. Once they arrived, 16 took half of the platoon to the top of a hill overlooking the village while SGT Brooks approached in the paddies. I was on the hill when we began to take fire. We were not allowed to fire into the village but began firing beside it and into the hillside. SGT Brooks was also firing around it and into the hill side. We realized it was his rounds hitting rocks that was getting us. I fired a burst 3 feet in front of him to get his attention. He radioed for us to adjust our fire. I told him I would adjust my fire on top of him if he didn't quit spraying the hill and he knew how good a shot I was. Now several of my friends were on board including Patterson, Lupichuk, and Wedekind and if he didn't quit I'd be forced to save ourselves. He quit.

Every mission we went on we took the tanks. Every mission we took the tanks one would get stuck and we spent the rest of the day getting him out, ending the mission. After a while Lt Brown ordered the tanks to stay and guard the camp and the ACAV's would pull the missions. After that we completed each mission with only once in awhile a track getting stuck. I thought Whitey was the best driver even though he would get stuck once in a while. One time Sarge jumped off the track to hook up the cable to pull us out. Rats swam towards the sergeant and I fired my M 16 to keep them off him. C-13 pulled us out-Whitey couldn't believe he got hung up.

Every morning I would go out to the make shift range and fire my 45 cal and M-79. I had little practice before coming over and wanted to be good with them. Lt. Mautua understood my concerns and gave his blessing. After a week I became an expert with both. The M 79 would drift 3 feet to the right every 100 yards. By studying this I soon was able to hit dead center what ever I shot at. I would prove this many times during my tour of duty.

10/15/1967, My squad was ordered 13 miles north up the beach to support some engineer's string telephone wire. While sitting around I spotted some fox holes and asked SGT Vernom permission to practice shooting at them. He said to ask the engineers who gladly gave their permission. The first round hit 3 feet above the hole but the second hit dead center. SGT Vernom said the first would have made the enemy jump into the hole and the second would have killed him. "Let me try". He missed by 10 feet, gave me the Blooper back (M-79) and said he'd leave it in the hands of an expert. I fired one more and again hit the hole dead center. I asked the engineers if they felt safe with us guarding them. "You bet," they replied.

That night their LT came running into our tent and told us that an MP jeep taking a VC prisoner to a navy landing craft had been ambushed. We loaded up and drove the 3 miles on the beach to in front of a large village. We hoped the whole village was not VC even with the fire power we had or we were in deep trouble. Lucky for us the VC had left leaving one MP wounded. The landing craft arrived and the MPs loaded their prisoner.

The rest of the week was quiet. Our tent, which was ½ tent and ½ poncho's, was under attack by a rain storm. SGT Vernom slept next to me under the ponchos. We noticed a large amount of water building up above where he was sleeping. We decided not to wake him. We watched the sag get bigger and bigger until it erupted, soaking him. He was jumping around and screaming why we hadn't warned him. "We needed a good laugh."

During our stay at Thunder Road we lost 1 APC and 2 tanks to mines in the sand.

Grant Coble

11/3/1967 to 12/15/1967, We were sent to the Pine Apple Forest for 1 ½ months following Thunder Road. We were in Charlie's back yard. Our mission was to offer support to the 17th Engineers and patrol during the day. Upon arrival we set up booby traps, trip flares, and clay more mines. I went to the engineers tent and the first thing I saw was a long hared, red headed guy with a flower shirt on.

"What are you doing here," I asked.

"I'm an engineer," was his reply.

Later we found out they were all "Pot Heads." I told the engineer I'd sure like to meet his LT. That night who walks into out tent? Yep! I recognized the LT from the firing range State Side. He had a case of vodka and one of whiskey. We got 2 bottles of each. I told him he'd had better trained us well as we were to cover his ass. It turned out the engineers, when stoned, worked very hard and well. When sober, they could hardly function. We later found out why they behaved the way they did. Booby traps, mines, snipers, VC attacks, and snakes had taken their toll.

Anthony John Newman, "Heads,"
Marijuana, Heroin, Obisital and Crank,
Opium derivatives, these we an all thank.
Provided to us with inscrutable ease,
To smoke, shoot up, and snort as we please.
A crutch to help us to the next light of day,
a numbing sensation for the legal murder we play.

Our first mission with the engineers we were shot at with a Thompson Submachine gun. We couldn't fire back, but had to get permission first. The VC was long gone by that time. I was really pissed off. The next day the same thing happened only this time I fired the M 79 at him. LT. Mautua yelled at me for doing this. I said, "I would not be a setting target for anyone and he could leave me in the rear if he didn't like it." After that everyone fired when shot at.

Two days later Lt Mautua, C-10, C-11, and C-14 went on a mission. Approaching an open field they spotted a squad of VC and opened fire, killing all. They captured several weapons including a Thompson Sub Machine Gun. The LT claimed the Thompson for himself. With the LT was Howie the driver, Miller, Saunders, SGT Hill,, Montaula, SGT Wright and 14 others whose names I've forgotten.

The next day Lt Mautau took the platoon out where we found a tunnel. He asked for volunteers but no one would. Finally Whitey said he would as he was small enough and crazy enough. I asked him, "By yourself?" I volunteered to follow him. Some 200 foot into the tunnel we found nothing. Returning the LT ordered us to blow the tunnel which became a trench once done. After that we were know as Tunnel Rats. We didn't mind it as down there we were our own bosses and what ever we found and wanted, we kept. This was the deal with command. We used our judgement when and if we'd shot down there. After that Whitey and I got away with a lot of stuff that would have gotten anyone else an Article 15. Maybe that's why we were the last to become SPEC 4.

Anthony John Newman, "Volunteer,"
Never volunteer I've heard them say,
but to be a tunnel rat, I did one day.
Lowered down on poncho liner,
For the lack of rope or anything finer.

Grease gun tucked beneath my arm,
assured me I'd not come by harm.
Inch by inch, to that thousandth yard,
Breath came shallow, swallowing hard.
Golden shafts of light came through holes,
In the roofs of tunnels, dug like moles.
One of two trip wires, cut with care,
Remove the mortar round and hand frag there.
C-4 explosives are shoveled in like coal,
Bangalores and shape charges, fire in the hole.
Fifteen minutes to run, not to get hit,
By mud and bamboo, all kinds of shit.

A couple of days later we came to a village and pulled a dismount. Half the crews went into the village while the others gave cover for

Grant Coble

us. I carried a 5 foot rod for prodding. At a straw pile I went to work when the LT came over and said he'd show me how to do it. With his new Thompson toy, he sprayed the pile. We all hit the dirt. The stupid Son of a Bitch was going to get us all killed. I asked him later what if there had been explosives in the straw? He would have wiped half of us out. Another stack was marijuana. We set that one on fire and moved back. Half of Vietnam was going to get high today. We found nothing during the rest of our search and returned to the tracks.

Our next mission, again 2 days later, was led by C-14, a tank. It crossed a hedge row and into an open area where the sand was lighter than the dirt around it and began to sink fast, up to the turret. We spent the rest of the day trying to get it out without success, breaking all our cables. We called for a tank retriever and was told not until the next day. So, we spent the night guarding the disabled tank. I asked the LT if we could set up clay-more mines and he said no. Could we shoot M 79 rounds every five minutes then and he said yes. The area we were stuck in was not a nice place and any VC could have sneaked in without being seen. This seemed to work for us. However some 3 miles away, about 2 AM, the base was getting hit. We could see the mortar rounds and RPG rounds hitting the base. We could hear 26 on the radio calling for fire support. Watching the gun ships circling, shooting rockets and machine guns was awesome. We were glad it wasn't us for they would have wiped us out. The VC crawled right up to the fence, placing bamboo poles over the trip flare wires and entered the camp in front of headquarters assigned area, throwing grenades at the tanks and APC's and into tents. Four guys were killed that night. Lucky for them half the grenades were duds. The battle lasted until sunrise. Some 50 VC were killed.

11/28/1967, Hillard Evans Williams, Ft Worth, TX, Friendly Fire, 31E/02

12/1/1967, Thomas L Motley, Buck Sgt. Quesenberry, Staff Sgt. Vernern and the crews of C-10, C-11, C-12, and C-13 got the orders to travel 150 miles south and pick up a 100 plus truck convoy. Sgt. Vernern commanded C-10 and C-11 and Buck Sgt. Quesenberry (Ques for short) commanded C-12 and C-13.

Dragoons

Ques was on my track, C-12, along with Harold Stephens (Whitey), Sarage, and Smithey. As we got into Tam Ky there was a 2 mile back-up of traffic. A truck had hit a mine and was in need of a tow truck.

We sat there in the middle of the market square, shortly after noon. I observed two teen age boys making their way through the crowd of villagers. I sat behind the driver, Whitey, and kept a very close eye on them. They were acting like I did at their age when I was about to get into some mischievous behavior. The one boy kept pushing and prodding the other. When the two boys were close enough, one threw a tin can at our track! Now, one's first reaction would be to shoot. But something told me to wait until the very last possible second.

As I observed the can in flight. I thought it was too small to hold a hand grenade. I prayed to God to "Please rotate" the can so I may see inside of it, and Lord behold if the can didn't rotate at the last second. The can was empty. I use the butt of my M-79 to knock the can back into the crowd and shook my head at the boys.

Just then the barrel of Quesenberry's M-16 came over my shoulder and pointed down towards the kids. I shoved the barrel into the air with my arm just as he fired, saying it was a prank and that I was doing my job as an observer and kept an eye on them. If the can had been an explosive device, I was ready to blast them with the canister round I had loaded and throw myself onto the explosive, to save my crew and the lives of those around us. I scolded the boys and told them how close they came to being killed. That if they ever tried that again, they may not be so lucky.

Once the road cleared, we continued our journey. It was around 7 PM when we pulled into the base camp, where the trucks were located. I felt it was too late for dinner, so several of us made up an "Irish Stew", C Troop style, with various cans of C-rations, Vienna sausages, and some "Hot" sauce. It really was delicious! The other troopers headed to the mess hall where they were served steak, mashed potatoes, gravy, beans, and cake. "Oh well", live and learn. Scout out the area before you react.

12/2/1967, We got ready to mount up. A total of 120 vehicles, 4 APC's, MP jeeps, and modified trucks. I ran down the line and told all drivers to make sure they had a full tank of gas. Once we went through the gate, we were going to travel at 45 MPH, or as fast as we could, and we weren't going to stop unless a vehicle got hit or disabled. We didn't want to give Charlie an easy target. I also made sure everyone was on the same radio frequency and locked and loaded. Once completed, I reported to Sgt. Vernern that we had a "Convoy" and we're ready to "Roll the wagons."

My track, C-12, was in the lead as usual. C-13 and C-10 scattered in the middle and C-11 brought up the rear. I liked being up front. I had a clear view of all the surroundings. With eyes of a hawk, I scanned the tree lines, shrubs, and the road for any signs of trouble. We kept in constant contact with C-10, C-11, and C-13 for slackers. It was a very tense ride as we rode 200 miles north to Danang. Anyone who had to go to the "Ladies room" either used their steel pots or hung it over the side. There were no rest areas.

We arrived shortly after noon at the gates of Danang. As the rest of the convoy passed us, they cheered and in some cases, saluted us. All 120 vehicles arrived safe and sound. Mission complete!

12/2/1967, Mike "Click" Colicchio, I remember the night like it was yesterday, and have recalled it almost every day of my life, since then. I had the first guard shift on C-20, about 2000 hours. It was one of those moonless nights in Vietnam, cloudy, with no stars either. The expression, "I couldn't see my hand in front of my face" was a reality. I held my hand out at arms length and saw darkness. C-20 was, to my recollection, about 20 yards from the wire, facing east.

There was quite a bit of activity in the area surrounding the base camp (small arms fire). I recall looking south, and in the distance, seeing red tracers going east, and green tracers coming west. Looking north, I saw the same. Gary Henspeter, C-20 Delta, relieved me around 2200 hours or so, and I recall saying, "We're going to get hit tonight." I went into the tent, took off my helmet, found a cot and went to sleep at the foot of the cot, with my feet on the ground, for some reason, half sitting and half lying down.

12/3/1967, At 0040 hours, explosions and shouting all around me in the tent. Someone shouted, "We're being attacked!" I said, "Fuck that, I'm tired!" I put on my helmet (remember, I hadn't undressed) and laid on the ground with my head in the center of the tent. Explosions all around, some coming closer, and lots of shouting. I thought it might be a good idea, at that point, to reverse my position, put my head closer to the sandbag wall, and my feet in the center of the tent, so I did. Within seconds, or so it seemed, there was an explosion at my feet. What felt like a slap, and was actually shrapnel from a Chi-com, Hit and penetrated my left buttock, and a hot piece of metal settled on my right, burning me slightly (actually hurt more). I looked up and saw the southeast end of the wall tent had been turned into a gaping hole, half the width of the tent. We had a single electric light bulb, still intact, which was emitting a bright beam and a great target for the infiltrator(s) who were lobbing grenades through the hole. I low-crawled to that spot in the tent, and prepared to vault over the sandbags. But there was the slight problem of the light and the grenade tosser, whom, I later learned, had been in the small wash that ran to the wire between our tent and the latrine, some ten yards sway. I yelled, to no one in particular, "Someone shoot out the light! Someone shoot out the light!" Mike Newland, God rest his soul, was on his back, under the light, with his M-16. Mike emptied a clip at the light. Still, there was a beam of light through the hole in the tent. Out on C-20, Henspeter was shouting, "I need some help out here! I'm running out of ammo!"

Now, I'm pointing at the light with my .45 and shouting, "Someone shoot out the light! Someone shoot out the ......", looking at my pistol, and feeling like a jerk. So, I took aim at the bulb and squeezed off a round; the bulb flickered and went dark. I thought someone had cut the generator, but the next day, in the hospital, I learned that the light had been shot out.

I figured Charlie's night vision had just been screwed up, so I counted to 5, and jumped over the sandbags. I ran to the track, handed up 4 boxes of .50 caliber ammo to Henspeter, mounted the right side M-60 and opened fire. I fired into the wire, in case any of our "guests" were still lingering. Apparently, the little bastards had taped the flares on the wire. My opening burst into the wire set off three flares, giving us some illumination (requests for illumination prior to this point had been denied). Gary Henspeter and Max Pryor, C-21, had caught, an killed, 8 of the attackers in a crossfire. I continued to fire into the wire and beyond, which was, by that time, purely recon by fire, as the attack had been repulsed. I fired until a cartridge ejected and jammed the slide on the M-60. I was switching guns when the order to cease fire was given.

That 45 minute firefight seemed like 30 seconds. Jim Warner dressed my wound, and that was the last time I saw Top Williams. He was securing the perimeter, and gathering the wounded for dust-off. He was wearing his steel pot, a flack jacket, skivvies, a pistol belt and jungle boots. A pretty comical visual, but a damn reassuring sight.

12/3/1967, Richard Charles Balukonis, West Hazelton, PA, Shrapnel, 31E/28

12/3/1967, Coleman Gee Hillman, Whiteville, TN, Explosive Device, 31E/27

Richard Hillman, son of Coleman Gee Hillman, wrote this poem the day his son was born, 7/17/1982.

For seventeen years he did his part,
He earned a Bronze Star and a Purple Heart.

But a VA check and Social Security,
Can't replace the life in his family.

Wham! Bam! Vietnam?
He fought for his country because he gave a damn.

I sure loved him, but won't see him anymore,
My daddy was killed in the Vietnam war.

Now I have a son that he'll never see,
but that's the price you pay when you want to be free.

Vietnam was a mistake, it was a lesson learned,
Lord help them all, especially the living that returned.

Coleman Gee Hillman

Wham! Bam! Vietnam?
They fought for their country because they gave a damn.

We sure loved them but won't see them anymore,
Too many "should have been daddies" were killed in the Vietnam War.

Well dad didn't leave me a lot when he died,
But I sure am glad that he left me his pride.

I'll agree with anyone that says war is bad,
but given a chance I would have died with my dad.

Wham! Bam! Vietnam?
Another life lost for Uncle Sam.

Dad gave more than should be allowed,
He gave his all and I'm damn sure proud

12/3/1967, Mike Collico, At daybreak, a chopper from Americal HQ descended on the camp; out pops a General (who is to me, and will remain, nameless as decency and protocol preclude my calling him what I feel is appropriate) who proclaims to "Top", First Sergeant, this base camp is a mess; why haven't you had a police call?" Now, I don't know and can only imagine what "Tops" response was,

Grant Coble

but, shortly thereafter, he was reassigned to an Infantry Battalion. The last account we had of him, First Sergeant Williams was being dragged away from a battle, by NVA soldiers; one of his hands had been shot off or cut off during the action. He died in captivity **(See date 9/16/1968).**

12/3/1967, Thomas Motley, That afternoon the tank retriever reached us and pulled the tank free of the mud. "You guys are lucky you were here last night". "Ya," we said, "Front row seats".

The Stars and Strips wrote an article about the battle stating an ARVN Ranger unit supported by engineers and an unknown cavalry unit killed 50 VC. We decided that was the last time we would be known as "Unknown."

When we got back to the camp I asked Whitey what had happened. We swapped our stories and it was then I got the nick name "Action." I was only trying to stay alive and the others around me.

Again, 2 days later we went out on another mission with us in the lead. Whitey was following the same tracks made by the 2nd Platoon the day before. I mentioned this to him and that the VC like to plant mines in the old tracks. He moved over 3 feet and continued on. C-16 asked us what we were doing and then ordered us back onto the old tracks. After some discussion he again ordered us to stagger the tracks. As we moved over again, turning to the left, our tracks dug up a mine which went off, blowing the front roller and track off. The roller went sailing over the rest of the platoon, I went 10 foot into the air, grabbing the radio antenna, pulling myself back down. I saw SGT Vernom go straight up an back down, landing on his 2x4 and breaking it. Whitey went 5 foot straight up, did a 90 degree turn and come down, setting facing me. C-16 called and asked what happened? Vernom told him we were hit by a recoilless rifle. The 6 foot hole under us said different. Whitey and Vernom were saying something and I asked why they were whispering. They weren't. The explosion made me deaf for a while. Koller was on the ground. "Did the explosion knock you off?" "No," he said, he jumped off. He mounted up in case of an ambush.

The medic put a bandage on a cut and asked me about my hearing loss. He wanted to report it to C-16 but I asked him not to for 24 hours. I was sure it would come back. A tank retriever was sent out for us.

The next day Whitey was ordered to go back to Hawk Hill and pick up a new track and to take someone with him. I went. We spent the next week re-arming the new track, checking fluid levels, installing new shields, and building ammo racks. When not working on the track we were free to do as we pleased. No guard duty or KP, just talk about getting back to the world.

Once the track was ready we went for a new radio, but there was no radio to be had. We decided to head back without calling ahead and let anyone know. On the way we planned on stopping at our first camp and paid our girlfriends a visit. Some grunt was hitch hiking and we picked him up. This gave us some extra fire power should we need it. The grunt thought we had it made. We explained this was our second track and what happened to the other. At the village he went on his way, Whitey his, and I to get some patch sewed on. Once done, I ran into the LT's driver. "What are you doing here?" "C-16 is here and we were on our way to get you guys from Hawk Hill." The LT showed up and asked where Whitey was and what I was doing here? I explained we had no radio and was on our way back. He wanted to give us an Article 15 for traveling alone, but didn't. Again being a tunnel rat paid off.

12/10/1967, Again we were on our way with C-10 in the lead and following the same tracks heading for the Pineapple Forest. The track commander became ill and was sent back. SGT Vernom took command of C-10 with Michael Saunders driving, Miller, and another who's name I forget. We were 4 tracks back and I was about to say something about following the same tracks when C-10 hit a big mine. Vernom was thrown into the air about 20 feet along with the others. Saunders was killed. Miller landed on his 45 and was paralyzed from the neck down. Ralph had a concussion and the other I know not what happened to him.

12/10/1967, Michael Jorn Saunders, Penacock, NH, Explosive Device, 31E/77

I was ordered to stay with my track and protect the area while SGT Wright went for help. Lt. Mautua called for a dust off and once the track was declared useless, munitions and weapons were removed. A case of C-4 was loaded on board and the track was blown up in place. Our mission was cancelled and we returned to base. Buck SGT Quesenberry became our new TC on C-12.

We jumped 10 VC running along the slope of a hill. SGT Quesenberry ordered me to lob an M-79 round at them but they were just out of range and it fell short. He opened up with his 50 and hit one dead in the back. I was watching with the field glasses and directed his fire. The rest of the platoon opened up and we got four. After that if anyone ran from us, we opened up. 2 hours later we spotted 13 VC in a paddy. 5 broke and ran and we finished them off, 3 men, and 2 women.

12/12/1967, It was early December and our Platoon was sent to Cigar Island to do some reconnaissance in a small village. C-16 informed Ques to take a small patrol into the village and search for signs of VC upon arrival. We spread out as we entered and began checking each hooch Entering one, I came upon a beautiful, fair skinned, red haired woman, in her 20's, of French blood, breast feeding her baby. I asked her to step outside. When Ques arrived, I called out to him and said, "See what I got! Can I keep her (jokingly)?" He said no an I asked her to step back into her hooch.

Suddenly a scream came from a near by hooch and I ran to it, weapon drawn. Entering it, I saw several young girls standing around a bed with an older Mama-son who had just given birth to a new baby. I lowered my weapon, took off my helmet, and showed the girls a picture of my baby son I kept in my wallet. This helped reduce the level of tension and fear with the girls and explained, "My baby-son." I looked at the baby and began to cry. I thought to myself, what are the chances of that baby surviving this war? It really got to me. This was the second and last time I cried; the first when I killed my first enemy soldier.

Walking outside the hooch, I called for the medic. He came running, wondering what had happened? I told him a woman had just given birth to a baby and to see what he could do for her. His reply was he had no idea for he'd never dealt with child birth. My reply was he knew more than me! Besides, the baby was already born. I showed the girls he was a medic by pointing to his Red Cross badge. When the medic left the hooch, he was all choked up.

When he reached Ques, he informed him of what he saw and that no VC were in the village. We loaded up, left the village, and returned to base.

Some engineers found tunnels and informed C-16 who yelled for Whitey and me. The tunnel I checked went in two directions so I dropped a grenade into it. After the blast I dove into it and went to the right. A small room contained a table, candle, and mat. There was nothing under the mat so I went in the other direction: nothing. Coming out, Whitey had checked the other tunnels and all were clear. The engineers went in, set explosives, and blew up the tunnels. The VC would dig some more some place else.

As the engineers continued to clear the forest they found mines, booby traps, tiger pits, and smaller pongee pits. A few days later as we worked the area C-17 threw a track. We and C-13 were ordered to the top of a hill to cover the area. The rest stayed for cover with C-17. The top of the hill was loaded with Tiger pits and pongee pits. We knew we were close to a VC base camp. Why else so much protection. C-16 refused our request to blow up the booby traps. I spotted a NVA soldier with a pouch on his side down the hill. I fired a M-79 round at him as he began to run but was not sure if I hit him in the bush. Dismounting, I headed after him but stopped after a distance and began to head back to my track. Suddenly I stopped! At my feet was a 6 foot long viper. Easing back, I pulled my 45 and opened up. The snake darted into the bushes. I continued to fire. Sarge and Quenesbarry came running over and opened up also. I began laughing. They thought I'd found a VC in a hole, but was only the snake. The Lt. wanted to know what we found and we told him we jumped a VC but missed. We saw the snake making "Tracks" over some rocks getting away.

We pulled out and were now the rear track and I was now rear guard. On a ridge I saw 3 people in black jump into some bushes. A 100 yard shot with the M-79, a hat flying into the air, and that was that. I didn't say a word to anyone. The engine noise covered the sound of the distant blast and my shot.

Smithy captured a mongoose and wanted to make a pet of it. He was crazy, I thought. One day it got loose and bit 8 guys trying to recapture it. Smithy, Whitey, and Rassel had to go to the aid station

Grant Coble

and begin taking rabbi shots. I took over as driver while Whitey was gone and Don Sergeant and Howie commanded the M-60's. Quenesberry was still the TC. We called Quenesberry "Quiz" for short.

With 8 guys on sick call and 5 more on R&R, we were restricted to guarding the engineers clearing the forest. The locals would come every day and haul wood for their homes and stockades for their animals. Koller stole a pig one night from a farmer who in turn told Captain Brown who in turn made us pay $20 apiece for the pig. With Thanksgiving just around the corner, we planned to eat well. The pig escaped one night, or was stolen, and we ate C-rations instead.

12/15/1967, Lt. Mantua became real sick and was sent back. The Platoon Sergeant, who we called carrot top, because of his orange red hair, was now in charge. We were ordered to a helicopter camp just north of Tam Ky. When not on duty we had some local girls come in and party with us. One, named Eva, 105 lbs., very sexy, had long black hair down to her hips. One of the guys lost his virginity to her and wanted to marry her and send her back home. We had to discourage him by proving she was prostitute. He was real upset when the full realization set in, but quickly got over it. All was cool after that. One night when we got back from a mission there were 50 guys standing in line waiting their turn. I was surprised by the number and he stated there were 100 at one time. $5 was the going rate.

Now, Eva was thought to be a VC spy so whenever she stayed over night we figured we were somewhat safe. Her friend Linda also would stay and we would party all night when not on guard. When she was nowhere to be found then we became nervous.

A helicopter dropped a load of 155MM rounds one day and C-12 and C-13 were sent out to retrieve them. We monitored the radio and listened as they were ambushed at the drop site. As they were trying to dig the rounds from the mud the VC opened up. Air support was ordered and after about ½ hour the crews were able to load up the rounds and return to base with no casualties.

12/17/67, It was mid December. Our platoon was stationed on the northern out skirts of Tam Ky. I was doing my turn on guard duty between midnight and 2 AM. I was observing the area around me when I noticed a white dog standing just to the left rear of my track. I watched the dog for several minutes. The one thing I noticed was that the dog never moved, not one inch, no tail waging or head movement. I called to him to see if I could get a response out of him. Still he didn't move. I turned my head to the front to observe the area in front of me for a few seconds and make sure everything was ok. When I looked back to the dog, he was gone! I looked all around for him, but to no avail. The area around me was all open ground except for the line of bunkers. I got on the radio and asked the other guys on guard duty if they could see a white dog running around be them? No was the answer. Now that dog couldn't have gotten away that fast! The guys on guard duty asked me what dog I was talking about so I told them what I saw. They all asked me what I was smoking down there? I replied that I don't smoke any of that stuff and I haven't been drinking either!

Soon Minx came to relieve me on guard. He asked me if everything was ok? I replied yea except for the white dog I saw and disappeared. He asked what dog? I said he was standing right over there! We turned our heads to where I pointed and to both of our amazement's, he was standing there again! In the exact same spot! I called to him once again, "Here boy! Here boy!" He just stood there perfectly still. I told Minx, "Now lets turn our heads away for a few seconds, then look again." We did and when we looked back 5 seconds later, the dog was gone. Minx and I looked at each other in disbelief! I said that I thought I was seeing things until you saw him also. Then I said that I'm not saying anything to anyone about this. They would think that we were both stoned out of our minds. The white dog was never seen again after that night.

Later in life when I told my wife Judy the story, she said that the white dog was my Spirit Guide and that he was probably letting me know that he was around keeping an eye on me and letting me know that everything was ok.

A mission, some 10 mile south of Tam Ky came up short one day in a traffic jam in town. Some one hit a mine south of town and we were stuck. It was market day and the place was full of people. We were on our guard with this many people around us. I watched

2 kids approach our track looking suspicious and acting funny. Getting close one threw a can at us and both took off running. The can turned in flight and you could see it was empty. We stopped them quickly and explained what they did was not cool. The next time we might kill them. Our mascot, Blair, a little black dog we had, was sick and Quiz was mad as the dog vomited all over the inside of the APC. He ordered us to get rid of the dog so we gave it to the kids. The villagers, knowing the seriousness of what had just happened were thrilled with the outcome. 2 hours later traffic began to move and the LT called off the mission. Back to camp we went.

SFC Wright became my new TC. From the start we did not get along too well. He was about 40-45 years of age, heavy set, and kind of a grumpy looking man.

12/24/1967, The XO came to our camp with a loud speaker mounted on his jeep. Just because we are in Vietnam, he was not going to let Christmas Eve go with out celebration. One man stayed with each track while the rest of us sang Christmas songs. The CB's joined in with us. Once this was over we broke out the beer and booze for some real celebrating.

12/31/1967, At midnight we opened up with M-60's and flares. We used all tracers for the M-60's and the sky was full of wonderful lights. No VC would dare come with in 2 miles of this madness. What a wonderful sight!

1968

1/3/1968, Captain Brown figured it was time for our R&R to be over and become soldiers again. We were off for Hawk Hill. Lt. King would become our new Platoon Leader. He was fresh out of West Point and had never seen combat before. He had no cavalry training either and would take the advice of "Veterans" until he got his feet wet. I guess 5 months of dodging booby traps, being shot at, and running over mines did make us veterans.

1/7/1968, C-12 and C-13 were ordered on a mine sweep. Lt King wanted to go along for the experience. We checked each bridge and any place we knew Charlie liked to plant mines. I ran the sweep and Whitey did the probing. We repeated the process back just incase Charlie sneaked in behind us and planted one as we passed. At the last bridge, a dirt filled culvert, we started the process when the Lt ordered us back onto the tracks. He felt there was no mine and was in a hurry to get back. We loaded up but did not like the idea. Later some marines came to our base and informed us they found a dud 105MM round at that same location and wondered what kind of a mine sweeping team we were. They also mentioned a track drove right over the dud. We let the Lt know in no uncertain words what they found.

We came under attack one night with rockets and motors while I was on guard. No one seemed to be responding from the bunker. Wright stayed with the track while I raced to the bunker to see what was going on. Not a soul was stirring. 2 shots with a 45 cal into the ceiling did wake them to action. Maybe a little too much partying.

The next day we went out looking for who shot us up that night and found them. SGT Wright was wounded in the hand and dropped into the ACAV for medical attention. I mounted the 50 cal and continued on firing. We sprayed the bamboo wood line heavy with suppressive fire and about ½ hour later all was over. 19 dead VC lay where they fell. Lt. King was getting his feet wet.

We again ran into the enemy the next day and this battle lasted longer and was tougher. We threw hand grenades into the trenches and the VC threw them back. Wright did a dismount with some of the other troopers while I manned the 50 cal. The Dinks were not budging so another stunt was tried. Using blocks of C-4 tied to common wire and a detonator inserted, lowered into the trenches, and set them off. Gun ships were over head also and working the area. When the battle was over some 40 VC were found dead.

1/21/1968, Our Platoon went back to Tam Ky and I to Eva. We were pulling guard duty and it was pitch black when someone a few tracks over yelled "Halt". There was no response. The track next to us yelled "Halt". No response. Then someone came towards our track and we yelled "Halt" followed by "Or I'll shot"! Lt. King quickly identified himself. He came to our track and wondered if we really would have shot. A sound "Yes" convinced him.

1/1968 Michael Prothero, Captain, Troop Commander

1/31/68,HQ, - A multi-battalion attack composed of provincial and local force units was launched against Tam Ky. The most significant intelligence gained from this engagement was that the enemy could coordinate and control an attack of approximately 2500 soldiers. Although heavy casualties were sustained, the enemy retained the capability to renew the conflict in the area in multi-battalion strength within seven days.

1/31/1968, *Tet Offensive,* **Thomas Motley,** C troop was attached to the Americal Division shortly after arriving in Vietnam in August of 1967. In January of 1968 our platoon was stationed in Tam Key, located north of Chu Lia, along with a Sea Bees unit, some 150 yards west of us, which was between our northern and southern line of defense. Our platoon consisted of 10 vehicles, 3 tanks and 7 ACAVS, or personal carriers. The tanks were C 14, C-15, and C-19 while the APC's were C-10, C-11, C-12, C-13, C-16 ,C-17, and C-18. Charlie 10 was the Platoon leaders track, or sergeants, and C-11 was the other half of his squad while C-12 and C-13 were the second squad. C-16 was the LT's track, or Lieutenant, while C-17 was the infantry's track and C-18 was the mortar track.

We had 47 men, of which 5 were on R&R. Lt King had split up our platoon into 3 sections, 2 APC's and one tank, guarding different areas. C-10, C-11, and C-14 were pulling bridge duty north of Tam Ky while the LT's track, C-15, and C-17 were on the north side of the perimeter. Charlie 18, the mortar track was on the east end and C-12, C-13, and C-19 were stationed on the south side of the perimeter along with 2 155 SPCs, or Self Propelled Guns.

It was about 4 AM when I went on guard duty. I was only on guard duty about 5 minutes when I observed a huge fire ball in the night sky. At first I did not know whether to wake the others or let them die peacefully for I was sure some one had set off a nuke. It was the ammo dump in Chu Lia and the beginning of the 68 Tet offensive.

I dismounted and ran into the bunker to wake my fellow crew members. I raced back to the track in time to hear C-10 calling C-16 and informing him that both ends of the bridge had just blowup. Rockets, mortar rounds, machine gun fire, and recoilless rifle fire started pounding our positions. As I watched, it looked like the Fourth of July. What a sight. Amazingly, not one round hit any of our tracks. At least 30 landed by C-18 while most of the rounds landed by the LT's tracks. I called on the radio to C-18 but no answer. It was at that moment that the TC came running from his bunker and mounted up with the rest of the crew in hot pursuit. At once they began using their 50 cal and mortar, letting the enemy know someone was home.

By this time our crew was mounted up. In the area in front of our track were 6 black clad VC heading our way. Pointing this out to Sgt Wright, I was ordered to open fire on them. My first burst landed short. A quick adjustment and one took the full load of one burst in the chest. The other 5 ducked for cover. Sticking up one's head was all I needed and he lost his mind. Another scooted for a building but another burst ended his quest. The other 3 disappeared.

We listened to the radio as Lt. King called for air support. Our side of the perimeter was not receiving fire while the mortar track and the Lt.'s section was. C-15 called to say his tank was hit by a recoilless round. The Lt.'s track also took a hit and was disabled.

Charlie 10 reported a Battalion of VC in a rice paddy about 200 yards in front of him and moving his way. They were carrying their weapons and waving flags as if they didn't have a worry in the world. The Platoon Sergeant ordered C-11 to fire at the end of the column while C-14 fired into the center and he would take on the front. They inflicted heavy casualties and the enemy broke and ran, abandoning their attack on our position.

All we could do was listen to radio reports as the fighting raged on. Around 7 AM we still had not received any fire. I radioed Lt. King to see if he needed any help? He said 'No ' and to maintain our position and guard the 155's just in case. I again called him and said, "At least let us send over C-19 as we didn't need him at this time." The Lt. said OK and C-19 pulled out. The TC began cussing me out. "The others need your help so quit bitching at me and go support them!"

Lt. King called us at about 8 AM to come and support his position. I asked the crews on the 155's if they would be ok? With a "Yes" we moved over to the northeast side of our camp near our old bunker which had taken a direct hit earlier that morning. The main gun was knocked out from a recoilless rifle. Charlie 13 set up in the middle. The LT's track, C-16, had taken a hit in the engine and could not move. Her crew still manned the guns, laying down cover fire.

We were receiving fire from the north side of our camp which had a 400 yard field of open rice paddies. At the edge was a tree line with a village behind it. About 300 yards out in the rice paddy was a dried up water bed that the VC used for cover to sneak up on us.

On the east side of our camp was the out-shirts of Tam Ky. This consisted of three buildings facing our camp in a parallel manner with two more perpendicular to them. The VC took up positions in these buildings. They also had snipers on the third floor of a building on the west side of our perimeter. One of the snipers had us pinned down good and almost shot SGT Wright in the foot. I asked for permission to take him out with my M-79 but Lt. King said we were not to destroy the building and that a squad of South Vietnamese soldiers were going to get the sniper. I replied, "Hell, by the time they reach them, we could loose a few good men!"

Later I saw a machine gun nest on the south east side of our position. Since I didn't have a clear field of fire from my track, I dismounted my M-60 and put it on top of the bunker located next to my track. This gave me an excellent shot at the machine gun but also gave the sniper an excellent view of me. With a new crease in the top of my helmet, I quickly dismounted the bunker. About this time the squad of Vietnamese entered the building to flush out the he or she sniper.

The firing began to let up a little. SGT Wright came up missing. Donald Wedekind motioned to the east where the sergeant had moved to about 75 yards away. He waved and indicated he needed ammo for his M-14. Grabbing a can of M-60 ammo, the same caliber used in the M-14, I ran to his location and we quickly took the rounds apart and loaded the ammo clips. He had seen some VC moving around some buildings and had moved to this location trying to nail a couple of them. Grabbing the Sergeants field glasses, I began scanning the area. I spotted a couple of VC running behind a building and out of sight. Grabbing the M-79, I launched a round their way. We watched the round arc over to them and land behind the hutch but never knew if we had hit anyone or not, but at least gave them a big surprise. Scanning the area some more, I spotted one individual hiding behind a stone wall with part of his leg sticking out. Relaying the information to SGT Wright, he took aim, about a 275 yard shot, and fired. Missed. "Raise 1 and right 2". Again firing, the Sergeant hit the target in the foot. We could see the soldier trying to hide himself better, but with out success. Another round and again a foot hit. The next round was a tracer and we hit a fuel can behind the soldier. The blast set the soldier afire and he scrambled from his hiding place. Ripping his field jacket off, we saw we had just shot a South Vietnamese soldier. He ran to a trench about 200 yards in front of us. We felt terrible and knew we had to do something to help.

There was still a lot of firing going on all around the area. Gunships flying overhead. The VC still controlled the buildings to our north and south. If we did not help this allied soldier soon he might not make it.

I began taking my helmet and flack jacket off when the Sergeant asked me what I was doing. "I'm going after him". "No, I will" said the Sergeant. "No, you're a much better shot with the M-14 and I can run faster than you," Was my reply, and I'll need you to cover me."

With about 150 yards of open field to cover - VC in front of me - CB's behind me and to the right - gun ships overhead - and a Sergeant covering me that really did not like me for personal reasons, covering me, I felt my chances were slim to minus something getting to the wounded ARVN. I paused and prayed to God that I'd make it and not catch a bullet from some direction. "Lord, please help me!"

As I ran towards the wire I saw some VC about 150 feet to my left heading for the CB's and opened up with my 45, emptying the entire clip. I realized they may have been out of range but felt better. Approaching the wire I looked for booby traps and saw it was clear. Climbing over the wire, I ran the rest of the distance to the wounded ARVN. He had his arms up so I would not shoot him. I bandaged his wounds as best I could, picked him up, and scrambled back to our position.

About 3\4 of the way back stood the Sergeant with his M-14. "What are you doing", I asked? "Thought you might need some help," he replied. He took the wounded soldier and carried him back to the CB's medic.

I took a moment to rest before getting back into the fray.

Grant Coble

Dragoons

Grant Coble

Thomas "Action" Motley some place in the Pine Apple Forest

Three guys were on board when I got back to the ACAV, George, better know as George of the Jungle, Donald Wedkekind, and Jim Lupichuk. They were using the M-60s and M-16s but not the 50. "Why?" "Not working right, only one round at a time." Checked it out and they were right. Tried adjusting the barrel but to no avail. Burned my hand doing so.

A VC was in the middle of the rice paddy so I loaded a round into the 50, a tracer, took aim and fired. Hit him squarely in the back and down he went.

Shortly afterwards, Donald and Jim dismounted and went to the LT's track to give him a hand. That left George and myself on C-12 to cover our right flank. Not having a clear field of fire because of the bunker, I dismounted my M-60 and put it in front of the track. "What are you doing?" George asked! Once explained, George dismounted his and joined me on my left. We had a mound of dirt in front of us for cover. I covered from 12 o'clock to 3 o'clock while George covered 9 o'clock to 12 o'clock, giving us a 180 degree of field of fire. About this time the radio crackled. George went back to answer it. Upon returning he said it was the LT. "And what did he want?" The LT wanted us to fall back and join what was left of the platoon. George's answer left a smirk on my face. "You fall back on us for we are not giving up our position in the face of the enemy!"

"Good for you George." I retrieved a case of hand grenades out of our track. "George, shoot anyone in front of our track." I figured there were no friendlys out in front and all were fair game.

We sprayed a tree line to our front in case the VC might try to regroup there. One hut in this location looked like a good command post and received some extra attention from us.

We were beginning to get short on ammo. Lucky for us SGT Barns and another Sergeant showed up in a jeep with some ammo that the First Air Cav left over when they moved out. Rusty as they may have been, we tried them and they worked. After this ammo was gone, all we had left was small arms and grenades plus what ever else we could improvise as a weapon. We had C-4 in the track to blow it up if need be and hopefully some dinks with it.

About 15 minutes later the LT called for air strikes. He told the 2 Phantom pilots from Chu Lia to make their strike about 100 feet in front of us and to be careful for some of his men were still on the line. The pilot told his wing man to stay close to his right side and in they came. We watched as the released napalm flipped end over end and covered our heads as they hit. What a sight!

After this things began to quiet down. Looking around I saw that only 3 of us were still manning our positions. Myself, George, and a tanker on a 50 cal. Guess the Dinks were taking too many losses trying to overtake us.

Taking advantage of the lull, I scouted around. One bunker had about 15 Dinks laying around it. The CB's had seen them race into it and opened fired at point blank with bazookas, blowing the hell out of everything. Sure was glad they were covering our left rear.

Perhaps a ½ hour later several of us were setting around our bunker when SGT Wright approached. "Come with me." He explained that we were going to police the area for unexploded rounds. "Why me?" "You like blowing things up," he replied. I tried to tell him blowing things up and picking them up are totally different, but to no avail. "Quit gripping," he said. "Ok, but stay close and you pick up the grenades and I'll pick up the mortars. If one blows up, I want you to be with me."

We gathered about 50 rounds and placed them in a ditch. I was never so scared in my life. Moving ever so slow and not tilting any for fear of jarring the firing pin. I placed two one pound sticks of C-4 on them and set the fuse. "Boom!"

We watched as other members cleared their areas and blew up the rounds. Two old Sergeants blew up their munitions only to have one round go straight up and come back down. I never saw 2 old farts get up and run so fast. What a funny sight to see!

The final tally was 2 KIA, 13 wounded, and 3 tracks knocked out. We killed over 150 enemy soldiers and an unknown number wounded. We learned later that we engaged a battalion and the bridge guard another battalion which was headed towards our position. I may not have been setting here writing this story and my name may have also been on that "Great Wall!"

1/31/1968, Jack Ray Lockridge, Piedmont, AL, Explosive Device, 2W/70

1/31/1968, Edgar Lee Bolding, Detroit, MI, Rocket Fire, 35E/87

2/1/1968, Thomas Motley, Some one star general landed in our AO. I asked him why he was here and he replied, "Want to see your R&R center." We all laughed and replied, "Right, R&R center."

For our actions that day we received the Presidential Unit Citation along with various other personal medals. I received the Bronze Star with a V Device for Valor for rescuing the wounded ARVN. And guess who put me in for a silver star- unhuh, SGT Wright. Learned later it was turned down because one more witness was needed.

It did amaze me, him putting me in for a medal. We still dislike each other, but respect each other for each other's courage.

2/7/1968, We returned to Hawk Hill for re-supply and new troopers for we had been mauled bad. I didn't get to know any of the new guys well. After loosing so many friends, a wall goes up, and new names and faces become non-existent. The hurt and pain is too much.

With 5 men on a track guard duty, starting at 8 PM and lasting until 6 AM, is 2 hours per man. I came from the beer hall and began my watch. About 10 PM, Wright shows up and informs me I have first watch. This was interesting as I was about done. Well, it wasn't, and for the next, almost 2 hours, I was still on watch. I glanced at the radio around 2345, nodded off, and woke up at 2400 (12 midnight). I heard one of my friends call my name. "They been trying to get you on the radio but no answer." Heading back to get SGT Wright up for guard I saw SGT Floyd and one of the tankers come around the back of the track but they didn't see me. Wright and I came out of the bunker and there stood Floyd wondering where I'd been. "Just waking the Sergeant for guard." I don't think he bought this as next day began my career of special details. After a week Lt. King told Wright to back off. This lasted one day before becoming a gate guard. A Troop ran into some trouble that morning and B Troop was called to help. Then C Troop went. Well, I had a job and as they passed, I smiled. That afternoon the unit returned with Wright setting at the M-60, all covered in mud. Later the driver, George, filled me in. As they crossed a dike, Wright was flipped off into the paddy. I felt satisfied.

Next morning I split at 6AM for the gate and the 4 Vietnamese hutches that supplied our laundry service to hide out. Some of the girls also supplied sexual services to supplement their income. I'd been there about 2 hours, sucking on some beer, when Jinx found me. Wright had been looking for me all over the place. Some trucks pulled up and about 30 GI's came in, all with one thing in mind. This was repeated once again and after about ½ hour they were on there way. Not too long passed and we heard some tracks pull up to the gate. Looking out it was our platoon pulling out for a mission. Jinx and I loaded up. Wright wanted to know what I was doing there? "Getting my laundry cleaned." Besides, they couldn't leave camp without coming through this gate.

During the mission, we found a tunnel complex some 300 foot long. No one was home and the LT wanted it blown. A case of C-

Grant Coble

4 did the trick and now there was a trench 300 foot long. Kind of looked like something from WW1.

That night back at camp we came under rocket and mortar fire. Very quickly we had 8 guys on our track, Whitey, Smithy, George, Wiedekind, Lupsichuck, Sergeant, Sergeant Wright, and myself . The Dink's motor rounds started where our oil dump was and began "walking" the rounds our way. I slid quickly into the drivers seat, catching a piece of shrapnel in the head doing so. You could see the flash of the mortar out in front each time fired. Starting the ACAV up, we backed up as the rounds closed. One round hit where we'd been sitting.

Anthony John Newman, "Lessons,"
Incoming, outgoing, you soon learn these sounds,
Learning to differentiate who's firing what rounds,
These are teachings, to survive you must learn,
Some only learn by death, or purple heart they earn.

2/19/1968, Micheal William Elben, Decatur, IL, Multiple Fragmentation Wounds, 40E/20

2/25/1968,HQ, Operations were planned in response to information received from the 72nd LF BN commander. C Troop was sent west of Tam Ky in the Pineapple Forest when action began, was ordered to move to the battle area, assume OPCON of the 3rd Platoon, B Troop, and to assault the enemy positions. The assault was begun at about 1630 hours with four armored cavalry platoons abreast. Assault fire was conducted with 50 caliber machine guns and M-60 machine guns. Shortly after 1700 hours the force reached the enemy position and dismounted personnel began to neutralize scattered enemy positions. The 6th ARVN Regiment had attempted to move into the enemy position during the assault, but received fire which forced them to withdraw. They were able to follow the attacking force into the position, and assisted in mopping up enemy resistance. By 1800 hours enemy resistance had been eliminated; 156 NVA bodies were counted and numerous weapons were captured.

2/27-28/68, HQ, Pineapple Forest , A report was received from the province advisory team at Tam Ky that approximately 35 wounded VC were located southwest of Tam Ky. After the engagement, a POW reported that his unit (72 MF BN) and several local force units were preparing to attack the ARVN military post at Chin Sung. The enemy forces were surprised by the cavalry and were forced to attack to avoid being overrun. After initial contact, the enemy's unit integrity failed and individuals fled, were engaged and defeated.

3/4/1968, James Kronner, I can't comment too much on the battle that started in early March 1968, I was only out in it 2 days. It all started when 1st Platoon was sent to occupy the hill to the north of Hill 29. This hill was by the back gate across from the large chopper pad. It was occupied by an Infantry Bat. But they were transferred somewhere else. We were too few to man the perimeter or bunker line so we formed a circle on the top of the hill. I was helping to pull guard duty on C-15 tank, as my tank, C-14, had already been turned in because of the damage it took in TET. We were awakened during the night when Hill 29 started getting mortar and rocket fire. I heard that there were no casualties from the attack.

3/5/1968, Next morning, the 6th, patrols were sent out to try to find the rocket launching sites. I did not go because I came down with a bad case of the GI's. The outfit got into heavy fighting out towards the western valley. SP4 Richard E Saldana was KIA. The troop came back in after dark then went out again next morning. Again I did not go out because I was still sick. After some running fights that day the troop stayed out all night on a hill top.

3/6/1968, Richard E Saldana, Saltburg, PA, Landmine, 43E/33

3/6/1968, Next morning, day 3, a tank from 3rd Platoon along with an ACAV from 1st went out with ammo to join the troop. I went on the ACAV as grenadier. We joined the troop which now gave it 6 tanks in the field and we moved out along with a company of infantry riding on top. We came up over a very rocky hill and faced another brush covered hill across a paddy. The tanks got on line and moved out into the paddy with the ACAV's filling in between and on the flanks and then we attacked the other hill. 1st platoon entered

Grant Coble

the brush on the right while the other platoons were still in the open. The NVA opened up on the exposed tracks knocking out one tank with a recoilless rifle an killing or wounding most of the infantry and 2 crewmen on another tank. Most of the rest of the infantry exited the other tracks and started back to the rocky hill on foot. After some initial confusion the CO ordered a retreat. SSG Arlie Terry and SP4 Jere Farnow were KIA. I was slightly wounded in the shoulder from a piece of shrapnel. The remaining 4 tanks shot up the tank that was hit by the recoilless and left it in the paddy.

3/6/1968, Jere Douglas Farnow, Las Vegas, NV, Small Arms Fire, 43E/18

3/6/1968, Arlie Terry, Fairborn, OH, Multiple Fragmentation Wounds, 43E/37

3/11/1968. Mike Colicchio, C Troop 1/1 Cavalry Regiment, Americal Division was in convoy on a road Northeast of Tam Ky in the Quang Tim Province of the Republic of Vietnam. My vehicle, C-20, was in the center of the convoy. An APC, from our 3rd Platoon, toward the lead element of the convoy struck and detonated an anti-tank mine. Upon hearing the explosion, I turned toward the sound and observed smoke and debris rising from the explosion. As the debris fell downward, the body of the, at the time, unidentifiable driver shot upward, twisting violently in the air. Years later I found out that the body of the Trooper that was blown from the vehicle was my friend Michael Garni.

It was, later, revealed that two individuals were KIA, as a result of that incident. They were PFC Henry B. Williams and Joseph Carlos Carvajal.. Henry and I were part of the same four-man training crew in Advanced Individual Training (AIT) in Ft. Hood, Texas. We trained on the same vehicle; slept in the same pod; we learned our military occupation specialty (MOS) together. For eight weeks Henry, Jackie Chamness, Bob Brothers, and I were inseparable. I was, and remain, deeply effected by witnessing Henry Williams death.

3/11/1968, James Kronner, Afterwards the troop returned to the hill where it spent the night before and the ACAV I was on accompanied the tank that lost half it's crew back to Hill 29. There I stayed until the 7th and last day of the fight. The troop had come back the evening before and the next morning it was decided that C-14's crew would take out C-15 tank to give it's crew a rest. While traversing a hill one of our ACAV's struck a mine killing PFC Henry Williams and Joseph Carvajal along with a number of infantry who were riding on it. After cleaning up, we moved on to another hill where we assaulted it suffering no further casualties. After this we returned to Hill 29 thus ending the 7 day running battle.

3/11/1968, Henry Braxton Williams, Jackson, Miss, Explosive Device, 44E/23

3/11/1968, Joseph Carlos Carvajal, Norvalk, CA, Multiple Fragmentation Wounds, 44E/15

3/12/68, HQ, - A captured document indicated that targets in the Chu Lai area would be attacked immediately. Hill 29 and Hill 35 received 45 rounds of 122MM rockets and approximately 50 rounds of mortar fire from the area west of Hawk Hill. Contact was made with a NVA force fighting from well constructed defensive positions consisting of reinforced bunkers, automatic weapons positions, and interconnecting trenches. All positions were well camouflaged and placed to take advantage of natural obstacles. Documents and POW's taken during the engagement identified the enemy force as the 3rd NVA Regiment, 2nd NVA Division.

3/15/68, HQ, A visual reconnaissance mission of Barrier Island indicated increased activity in the area of Ha Binh (vic BT2445). OB listed three local force companies and one main force battalion operating in this area. After contact was broken, no identification could be made of the force encountered.

3/15 to 4/9/68, HQ, Intelligence indicated increasing enemy activity in the mountains along route 533 west of Tam Ky to Tien Phouc. Air recon missions revealed numerous fortified positions and a great deal of night activity. Agent reports indicated that this area was being used as a base camp for several District force units and reports from returnees indicated several supply caches were maintained in the area for NVA forces.

4/2/1968, Thomas Motley, I was on the truck that was transporting me to the air base, when we came upon the incident. I thought it was in late March when they hit the mine, not in April as people said. Jim Lupichuck was the TC on the track (C-13). As we pulled up, I saw Jim standing there with several other troopers. I saw Rassells body being covered up, It happened on their way back from their mine sweeping duty that day. The VC apparently planted the mine after C-13 made their first sweep and waited for them to get out of sight, then they must have planted the mine in the road. On their way back to camp they hit the mine. I knew that some day this would happen because the local villagers would watch us everyday as we performed our mission.

They knew we were creatures of habit, so it was easy to figure out a way to get to us. Hell!, if I was a VC, that's exactly what I would have done. That's how I survived 8 months in C-Troop. I trained myself to think like the VC and to anticipate what they might do.

4/2/1968, Robert Herman Rassel, Waubun, WA, Landmine, 47E/42

4/2/1968, Bruce Lyle Badger, Danville, VT, Multiple Fragmentation Wounds, 47E/40

4/2/1968, George John Kohlmeir III, Binghamton, HY, Landmine, 47E/38

4\8\1968(7/30/2003), Mike Colicchio, Mike was about to become a father. He was offered the chance to go home to see his daughter, but elected not to when informed he might not be able to return to C Troop 1/1 upon returning. He therefore stayed on and was transferred anyway to a new unit, or as we would say, demoted to the 9th Division. He never saw his baby girl. When she was born, it was like the entire platoon became fathers; we all shared in the joy, in that hell hole. Some of us have been devastated for years by his death.

Through the efforts of Sonia Clark, Kelly Michele Newland was contacted on Fathers Day, 2003. Kelly, her mother, Carol (Newland) Donnano, and Kelly's family, Husband Shawn, and daughters Brook and Lizzie, all attended the C Troop Reunion at Fort Knox, Kentucky on Labor Day weekend. 2003. The resemblance that Kelly, Brook, and Lizzie had to Michael Dwaine Newland, their father and grandfather, respectively, was phenomenal. It was as if "The Duck" was there among us, physically, as well as emotionally.

4/8/1968, Michael Dwaine Newland, Lima, OH, Landmine, 49E/04

4/9/1968, 0600 hours, HQ, A Troop plus one platoon of C Troop departed Hawk Hill with the mission of clearing Route 533 from Tam Ky to the Tien Phuoc NFZ. At 1224 hours, Tm A had linked up with 2nd platoon, D Con, 26 Eng, and moved to construct a bridge site (vic BT211167). C Troop conducted an area recon (vic BT197183) with moderate contact.

4/10/1968, HQ, A Troop conducted an area recon (vic BT190170) with light contact while C Troop conducted an area recon (vic BT199188) with no significant contact.

4/10/1968, The 2nd Platoon, C Troop, 1/1 Cavalry, Americal Division was conducting a search and destroy mission west of Tam Ky in the Quang Tin Province of the Republic of Vietnam. The Platoon came upon a creek bed and, subsequent to a reconnoiter of the area, proceeded to cross the creek bed. After 2 APC's had crossed the creek, my vehicle, with PFC Willie E, Glover, PFC Allan D. Hanlan, SPC 4 Kimmey D. Hobbs, Lt. Ronald J. Wojtkiewicz, and SPC 4 Quillard F. Lyons on board, proceeded across. I was in the command seat, with Lt. Wojtkiewicz and the rest of the crew in the rear hatch. The "track", C-26, climbed the steep embankment, and slid back down. Upon doing so, C-26 detonated an anti-tank mine. I was blown clear and landed in the pool of water adjacent to the crossing, sustaining a ruptured spleen, a pneumothorax, two compression fractures, and a superior fracture of the spine. The driver, SPC 4 Lyons and I were evacuated, and the rest of the crew were dead. While in triage, I was administered the Last Rites of The Roman Catholic Church indication that I was in grave condition. After an undetermined time, I awoke in post-op and saw Lyons across the ward from me. Some time later, I heard a nurse calling his name and slapping his face, attempting to wake him; I opened my eyes, briefly, and fell back to sleep, as she continued. When I awoke, again, Lyons was not in his bed; no one responded when I inquired about his whereabouts. He and the rest of my crew are on **Panel 49E, lines 10,11, 18, and 44, alphabetically, on the Wall.**

Approximately one month after this incident, while recuperating at a hospital in Japan, I flashed back to the river crossing and remembered something that has disturbed me ever since. I distinctly remembered two of our NCOs, SSGT Jim Wanner and another SSGT, I think his name was Robinson, but I can't be sure, were standing on the top of the embankment, their vehicles having successfully negotiated the crossing. In front of them, and at the edge of the embankment, were criss-crossed branches, exe (XXXX), all along the embankment.

At the Americal Leadership Course that I had just completed in Chu Lai, we were taught that was a signal, left by the Viet Cong, warning the local population that the immediate area was mined. I saw it; I should have remembered; and I should have prevented five deaths. I didn't, and I revisit that embankment and relive that incident everyday, when I wake up with a pain in my spine every morning, and recall how that pain came to be. "Survivor Guilt?" Probably. Guilt? Definitely.

 4/10/1968, Willie Edward Glover, Marietta, Ga, Landmine, 49E/10

 4/10/1968, Allen Dewey Hanlan, Cleveland, OH, Landmine, 49E/10

 4/10/1968, Kimmey Dean Hobbs, San Antonio, TX, Landmine, 49E/11

 4/10/1968, Quillard Frank Lyons, DeRidder, LA, Landmine, 49E/44

 4/10/968, Ronald Joseph Wojtkiewicz, Omaha, NE, Landmine, 49E/18

 4/13/1968, Richard Alvin Renfro, Kanasa City, MO, Multiple Fragmentation Wounds, 49E/47

 4/29/1968, Harold Henasey, Burlington, NJ, Explosive Device, 53E/01

 4/29/1968, James Willard Powers Jr, Loyalhanna, PA, Explosive Device, 53E/06

 5/5/1968, Jerry Frost, Captain, Troop Commander

 5/5/1968, Stephen M Lashinsky Jr, Newton Square, Pa, Rocket, 55E/20

 5/15/1968, George Herman Coppage III, Wyoming, Delaware, Small Arms Fire 60E/21

Anthony John Newman, "The Chaplain at Tea,"
Chaplain Lamback, I remember you well,
We had tea together a little east of Hell.
Smoking an joking for all it was worth,
Up comes the Chaplain, smiling with mirth.
"Join us for a spot of Tea?" Limey inquires,
Just put the steel pot on over the fires.
Biscuits and Crab, Mushrooms and Cheese,
Shrimp for the taste buds, so different, to please.
The Limey religious? I'd only be lying,
But Chaplain thank you much, for comforting the dying.

6/1/1968, Thomas Lynn Butler, Monroe, Kentucky, Small Arms Fire ,62W/20

6/1968, Carl Wronko (Authors note: The time frame of this story was written in its entirety including time not spent in Vietnam), I had graduated from Rutgers University in June of 1967 and had decided to go to Law School after college for no particular reason. After my first year I needed a break from school. I'd never worked in a full time job: and , I was still living at home sleeping in the same room that I had since I was a teenager. Well, what to do? A friend of mine from college by the name of Steve Shore had decided to join the Army and sign up for Officer's Candidate School. Now mind you the Vietnam War had been going on for just about two years at this time and it didn't take a learned man to figure out that a stint in the Army would very likely include a tour of duty in Vietnam. The Country itself was becoming more and more divided over the war and it just wasn't the patriotic thing to join up, at least not in the New York Metropolitan area, and North Jersey is definitely part of that area.

Well, I decided that the Army was for me and that it would be a great change of pace in my life. So, in June of 1968, Steve and I went down to the Army recruiter in Newark and signed up for the Army with a promise of Officer's Candidate School. My folks were not thrilled when I told them - looked at me like I was out of my mind. Both my parents had been through World War 2, my dad having served in the Army Air Force, and my mother having married him during that time. My mother's brother had been badly wounded while serving in a tank crew in General Patton's Third Army. They knew what was in front of me. They were part of what would be later called The Greatest Generation.

Steve and I decided we'd opt for a Delayed Entry into the Army and didn't have to go until the end of the summer. Well summer at the New Jersey Shore went really fast and the end of September came around even faster and before you know it, it was time for physicals so we went down to Newark at the Federal Building to take them. I failed for high blood pressure and they were going to turn me down. Now all around me, guys are trying everything to fail that physical to no avail and here I am, wanting to get in the Army, and I can't pass the test. Prevailed on the nurse to let me lie down and rest for a while and then take the test again. Well after two tries, I pass. Great, I'm in the Army. Why is there a little voice in my brain saying, "Stupid, you could have gotten out of that whole thing."

One week later we board buses for Basic Training. Don't know where I well be sent but say long good byes to my family as I don't know when I'll see them again. Get on a bus and get taken about two hours away to Ft. Dix. Put in temporary barracks and await training. My family comes down on Sunday. Long good byes wasted. Well, I spent my time in Basic Training at Ft. Dix: and, when that is done, I sweated out the next assignment location which turned out to also be at Ft. Dix where I was assigned to Advanced Infantry Training. During AIT, I began to get the idea that the Army was taking this Vietnam stuff serious as we surrounded and searched villages made of bamboo and leaves in all types of snowy and icy weather in the New Jersey winter. Next, after AIT is over, the Orders came down for OCS and I was on my way to Ft. Benning, Ga. Home of the Infantry and my home for the next six months. I went without my buddy Steve Shore who incurred a hernia picking up an M-60 Machine Gun during training and ended up spending his entire Army Career as a Spec. 4 in the Intelligence Branch at Ft. Meyers, Md.

At Ft. Benning, I'm assigned to the 95th Officer Candidate Company and now begin to experience the seriousness of the Army's training of its future officers. It gets progressively more challenging, both physically and mentally tougher. I get to experience leadership training in a big way, the Army way - give you a class on the subject and then throw you into it with all types of graders and checkers looking on. Well, I get the swing of things and do well in class and in the other training activities. Just prior to graduation in July of 1969, I and two other Senior Officer Candidates are called into the Company Commander's Office to be told we finished in the top three in the class entitling us to some career choices. We can have a Regular Army Commission in the Infantry: or, we can have a Reserve Army Officers Commission in either the Signal Corps or the Armor Branch. We are given several days to think about it. During the next few days we go through a combined arms exercise with Tanks and Infantry training together. I get to ride on a Tank, Commander's position no less, and watch my OCS buddies in the Infantry mode, running to keep up in the hot Georgia summer. This impressed me. That night I think things over as I have to decide in the morning. I reason that I'm not interested in a career in the Army and going to Vietnam as an Infantry Platoon Leader can be unhealthy, so that option is placed aside. Leaves me with Signal Corp or Armor Branch. I sure did like riding on that tank: and, ever since I was a kid I was fascinated by armor. Didn't think they had tanks in Vietnam and reasoned that I'd probably be sent to Germany. I later learned that this was very faulty reasoning based on lack of information. In Vietnam, the Signal Corp types are often placed on lightly defended hilltops and that is dangerous: and, besides, what do I know about Radios. So, I'm going to be a tanker. I graduate Ft. Benning School for Boys as a brand new Butter Bar Second Lieutenant of Armor and I'm feeling fine.

7/23/1968, HQ, - The 1st Squadron 1st Cavalry was in contact with an unknown size enemy force (vic BT1528), 13 kilometers east of Nui Loc Son. Documents captured in this contact identified the GK-40 Engineer BN, 2nd Division.

7/23/1968, Joel Alvin Jefferson, It was just another day in Nam. The day started out like any normal day. First thing that morning I had chow and then took a walk down the hill where we all lined up. Our tanks and APC's went out into the field as they did any other routine day. The place we were headed for today was Pink Vill. We often went there on recon looking for Charlie.

On this particular day, I was riding on top of the lead APC(or track is what we called it) and talking to the other M-60 gunner. I don't remember his name. We always got replacements as someone was always being wounded or being rotated back to the world. All of a sudden, we hit a mine and I was in the air looking down at the APC as I fell back to the ground. The other M-60 gunner was blown up and off the APC too.

Pink Vill was very sandy, something like a beach, so the ground was soft. When I landed, I didn't hit the ground as hard as I thought I would. I was hurt form the fall, but mostly from the noise from the concussion of the mine.

The Track Commander(TC) was killed and the driver was under the APC down in the sand. The APC was upside down. We spent most of the morning, or afternoon, I can't remember which, looking for the TC's lower body parts in the sand. That was the first mine explosion I was involved in that day.

The second mine explosion happened when I was riding a VTR(Vehicle Tank Recovery) that was pulling my APC back to Hill 29, or Black Hawk Hill. I was riding on top of the VTR in Pink Vill when we hit another mine. We had just started moving slowly because of the sand. This time everyone was running all over the place, shouting, "Get off the VTR!" It ran on gasoline and could have exploded since it was flammable. The VTR didn't fly up in the air like the APC did, but the explosion was just as loud and the sand got into my eyes and I couldn't see for awhile. My ears were already ringing from the first mine and this time they started to bleed from the blast. I made it back to the hill alright, and was rushed to the Field Aid Station with running eyes and bleeding ears.

I didn't leave Vietnam after getting hurt. I was put in HQ Company in GSR until I healed up and then I went to work in the ammo dump driving a five-ton truck. I was in charge of the truck and responsible for bringing ammo from Chu Lia's ammo dump back to Hill 29.

I never left Charlie Troopers because Perry Antoine and the rest of the guys in Charlie Troop were like family. I'm not saying I

Dragoons

wasn't close to some of the guys in HQ Company, because I was, but HQ wasn't a field unit.

7/23/1968, Pete M Harrington, Ken was the Tank Commander of C-10. First Platoon had the Pink Ville duty on the 22nd. That was when a Platoon would rotate down to Pink Ville, spend the night, make a sweep in the AM and usually return to the hill the next day after another Platoon relieved them. I think this was rotated between all Troops, A, B, and C with a Platoon down there every night.

Pink Ville was located just south of Tam Ky, not the one down Quang Nai area. The morning of the 23rd, we started the sweep. Butler, the TC, a guy all I remember as Slick (might have been Washington) as right gun, I on the left gun, and a guy that had rotated up from down south, 4th Infantry. I think Larry was driver. We were tracking a lead Tank and hit a command detonated mine. Ken was killed instantly. They dusted us off to LZ Baldy. Ken was a good man and I would have definitely enjoyed meeting with him when we got home. I met a local fireman from his home town years later. He told me the whole town kind of shut down upon hearing of Ken's death.

7/23/1968, Kenneth Allan Butler, Kalamazoo, Mi, Explosive Device, 51W/38

8/12/1968, Bradley Joseph Simmons, Ancrandale, NY, Explosive Device, 19W/23

8/23/1968, Edward Samuel Stewart, Pensacola, Fl, Multiple Fragmentation Wounds, 47W/55

8/23/1968, Richard Lee Rowland Jr, Phoenix, Az, Multiple Fragmentation Device, 47W53

8/24 to 27/1968, HQ, Enemy units identified in this contact were the 1st MF Regiment and elements of the 3rd and 21st NVA regiments. It was estimated that there were 1200 to 1500 enemy in the contact area. The enemy was well dug in throughout the contact. The positions were principally in the hedge rows on islands of high ground which were surrounded by rice paddies. At 1227 Hours while moving into the area of contact C Troop received AW (Automatic Weapons) and RR (Recoilless Rifle) fire (vic BT232223). The troop was able to suppress this fire with negative casualties and continued to the river ford (vic BT231218), crossed and linked with A-26

Grant Coble

assuming OPCON of this element. A Troop arrived 45 minutes later and assumed command of A-26. The two troops now began extending to the left with C Troop on the north and A Troop on the south. Continuous AW fire and RPG fire was coming from the enemy positions. Throughout the afternoon of the 24th the Squadron had been asking for an infantry company to combat assault into the area. At approximately 1630 Hours the Squadron received word that one Company would be available at 1700 Hours. An LZ (Landing Zone) was selected (vic BT228218) and C Troop was given the mission to move into this area and secure it. Upon moving into this area C Troop came under the heaviest fire of the day. The lead elements were forced to "Circle the Wagon" and returned fire 360'. It was apparent that this was not a suitable LZ and the rifle Co B-4-21 was diverted into Hawk Hill. A second Rifle Company was also diverted to Hawk Hill. Due to the lateness of the hour the two troops began to disengage from contact and move to night logger positions closing into these positions at approximately 2300 Hours. Results of the first day o the battle were: 227 NVA KIA while friendly losses were 2KHA an 23 WHA.

8/24/1968, Donald R Pyrant, Sanford, NC, Small Arms Fire, 46W/07

8/24/1968, William N McMurtrey, Killen, AL, Explosive Device, 46W/06

8/24/1968, John Ahrenberg, We are pulling mine sweeping duty from Hill 29, our base camp. I drove an M-48, A-3 tank. What a great tank it was; take a licking and keep on ticking. Mine duty was the worst duty one could pull. How does one fight a mine? Can't see it. No one to shoot at. Nothing to defend. I personally hated it. You just kept creeping along behind some guys sweeping the road with mine detectors hoping they would find the mine laid the night before. And oh how they liked to lay mines! Funny how I remember all the debris laying along side the road as a testament to how well they laid mines. Their favorite was, or as we called it, a Nitor Starch bomb. The VC melted down the insides of a bomb, separating the nitro, and then mixing it with buffalo dung to stabilize it. Then they put in a blasting cap and bamboo detonator, dig a hole in the middle the road, and plant it. Run over the blasting cap and

"Bang!" I hit one once on Highway 1, a dirt road, and blew all the road wheels off one side, warping the hull so bad they replaced it with a new one.

So, here we were crawling along behind the mine sweep crew. Once the road was cleared, we declared it so and returned to base and guard these guys during the night. Next morning the process would start all over again. This duty only lasted for one week and then another team would rotate to replace us. We "Hated" this duty.

8/24/1968, 3rd Platoon came into heavy contact with the enemy. We gathered around Lt. Wassons track and listened to the chatter on the radio. I was worried as a good friend, Johnny Occhilline, was in the 3rd. We grew up together and joined the Army together. Moments later we received the call to mount up and move out. We were heading for the Pineapple Forest and help our brothers in need. We hated this place. It was close to the Loas boarder and all the enemy had to do was cross an invisible line and they were in our back yard.

We knew it would take most of the day just getting to the 3rd's location. During the trip a scout track hit a mine which killed several of the crew members. Us tankers called the APC's "Coffins" because when they hit a mine someone almost always lost their life.

8/25/968, HQ, The plan for the second day of the fighting was to place one Cavalry Troop to the west of the enemy position in a blocking role, and attack with two troops and the two Infantry Companies, which were lifted into the logger area on the morning of the 25th. In order for B Troop to move intact from Hawk Hill to its blocking position, it was first necessary to bring its platoon which had been securing Sparrow Knob back to the Hill. This was accomplished in a pre dawn march and B Troop was able to SP at 2016 Hours. After completion of re-supply A Troop moved west to the area of contact on 24 August. C Troop was given an objective, center mass (BT215221). Five preplanned airstrikes were flown prior to the initial assault. As on the 24th, A Troop received intense AW/RPG fire from the trench lines on its objective. However, the availability of the Infantry made it possible for A Troop to move into its objective area. Before A Troop was able to entirely split the objective, darkness once again forced the Company to disengage and move to night logger position. Meanwhile C Troop, to the north, had encountered positions that had been left untouched during the fighting on the 24th. In the initial assault of the objective the C Troop met stiff resistance in the form of a reverse sloop defense. The assaulting Infantry had progressed too far in advance of C Troops ACAVs masking their fires. Portions of the Infantry were pinned down for a time but successive assaults by the ACAVs and tanks finally succeeded in their relief. C Troop was forced to disengage in order to bring in dust off. Immediate airstrikes an gunships worked the area over while C Troop evacuated its wounded. It was B Troop, however, that found itself in the worst predicament of the day. While moving south B Troop encountered enemy entrenchment's as far north as (BT2025) and (BT210238) . B Troop received heavy RR, RPG, an small arms fire. This position was believed to be held by an NVA Battalion. One platoon was left to engage this position while the rest moved on to its blocking position (vic BT217210). It soon became apparent that there was no need for a blocking force because the enemy, at this time, was not inclined to leave his trenches. B Troop found its proposed blocking position occupied by what is believed to have been the Regiment HQ's. B Troop assaulted into this position an soon found itself in the middle of the position receiving fire from all sides. Once again A Troop was forced to form a perimeter and return fire 360'. The 3rd Platoon of A Troop was ordered link up with its parent unit when it was determined that they would be of greater value in that location. The team stayed in its position throughout the afternoon leaving only when the light began to fade. It is now felt that this assault so disrupted the command structure of the Regimental HQ that it was withdrawn the night of 25 August. All units began disengagement from contact at approximately 2330 Hours. The only team experiencing any difficulty was A Troop which continued to take RPG fire having 2 ACAVs hit, one of which had to be destroyed in place. This brought to two the number of combat loss vehicles for the battle. C Troop having had a mortar carrier detonate a mine while moving to its night logger on the 24th. One dust off helicopter was destroyed on the 25th after it was shot down inside of B Troops position. The crew and wounded were all evacuated by a second helicopter which took several hits including one RPG round. This helicopter was forced down east of the battle area and subsequently recovered. There were 9 sky spots flown against the objective during the night of 25-26 August. Results of the second day of the battle were 259 NVA KIA.

8/25/1968, After the dust off we continued on until finding the 3rd and I found the "Big O". This was Occhilline's nick name. He was really shook up. After seeing Johnny's tank and listening to his story I could see why. They had blindly driven into the middle of an NVA regiment and had to fight their way back out. His tank had been hit by 3 RPG's-chewed up by a Russian 51 cal, leaving ½ inch holes and dents all over the tank. The brackets holding the lights on and the periscope used by the TC when buttoned up were all shot up. They lost a lot of tracks that day. Enough that the 3rd supported and covered our rear for the next 5 days. A lot of good men were either killed or wounded that day. I was scared. "Oh ya, I was scared!" If someone had told me they weren't, I'd have said they were either crazy or insane, or a little of both.

We spent a sleepless night knowing what awaited us the next morning. We spent the night on a little knoll some clicks away from where the Big O Platoon had engaged the enemy. We knew this was something big as all of 1/1 was sent into this area. I had never seen this before. Looking back I wonder if our commanders knew what was in store for us the next morning. If they did they didn't share it with us. Knowing now how many NVA regulars where in the area, it was a good thing we didn't know. What we did know after what 3rd platoon went through was that some of us would not be alive after this encounter. Like all the troopers before us, you just suck it up and do your job.

In the morning a group from the 21 Infantry Division flew in to support us. Now this isn't anything new to us. I sat in the dirt away from the dust those dam choppers blew up when some grunt walks by the back of the tank. I looked up and thought I recognized him from my home town of Surprise, Az. "Nicky," I said half heartedly. He didn't hear me so I repeated his name again louder, "Nicky!" He turned around and sure enough it was Nicky Bacon from my home town. We gave each other a hug and said about the same thing, "What are you doing here?" Neither of us knew the other was in Vietnam. We held a reunion right on the spot. Years later we pondered the odds of us meeting someplace like Nam during the same battle among some 500,000 GI's from the same small town of 1,000. You would have had better odds winning the lottery. Little did we know how this meeting would change our lives years later.

Several hours later we began to move towards the location the Big O encountered the NVA the day before. It was one of the hottest days any of us could remember. Several Grunts passed out from heat exhaustion and were dusted off. Nicky's patrol went into the brush and within several minutes made contact. We could hear machine gun fire and explosions. Lots of explosions! CONTACT! We drove into the brush from the paddies and engaged a force. I had never seen so many NVA regulars and so well dug in. They had bunkers and trenches everywhere. We drove up the hill to rescue the grunts when we came under intense fire from all sides. There were thousands of them; thick as ants.

I saw a 105 recoilless pointed right at us. My tank commander and good friend, Roy Ames, fired a canister round and took it out. They came out of the trenches and fired what seemed dozens of RPG's at the same time. There were so many you didn't know where to fire so you fired everyplace. This one NVA regular laid in a hedge row so close I could see his eyes (I swear) and fired his RPG. The round hit our front slope and ricochet into the dirt.

Nicky's guys were on both sides of us dying like flies. I saw his LT get hit in the head, then his sergeant. We were firing as fast as we could load the main gun but it was almost impossible to hit someone as well entrenched as these guys were. We fought like this for hours, taking ground, then being pushed back. We exhausted our supply of main rounds and had to fall back to re-supply. Air strikes were called in. Usually this is very effective but these guys were dug in too well. Nicky's guys were taking a beating. They had lost dozens in this first engagement. Nicky took charge of what was left of his platoon.

Several hours later we again attacked the enemy. We could see many bomb craters, but few, if any hit their mark. The NVA were just as strong and as well armed as before. Nicky's men were again on both sides of us getting pounded. He stood up, machine gun rounds hitting the ground in front of him, and pointed for his men to go to the left and right. I knew that at any moment he would be killed and there wasn't a thing I could do for my friend. Suddenly he attacks the NVA positions, firing his M-16 and tossing grenades into bunkers. I put the tank into forward and we did a C-Troop charge right into the middle of the action until we were driven back by intense RPG fire. The order came for us to fall back as it would be getting dark soon and we were running low on ammo.

Several clicks isn't much for a night time defensive position when this close to an enemy force of this size, but we took what we could get. None of us slept well that night. Several tracks had been knocked out and many men were either dead or wounded during the action, most of them Nicky's.

We advanced the next morning expecting to find the NVA in disarray. No such luck as they were dug in better than ever. We called in air strikes over the next several days with little positive results. A and B Troop did not fare any better than us. We couldn't see them due to the trees and brush. We repeated the process of charging and falling back for several days. Re-supply and charge again. During one charge several grunts were killed or wounded in front of us as we pulled back. Nicky asked us to go back in and get his dead and wounded out. I learned in the Army you do not volunteer for anything, except this was different. We weren't about to leave our fallen brothers up there so we charged again (for the uncounted time again). Upon extracting our guys, we fell back to another nightly defensive position and another night of little sleep.

Anthony John Newman, "Bringing Out A Buddy,"
Forged by fire,
A friendship so strong,
Even death won't stop it,
When one of us is gone.
Through pain and misery,
I will surely strive,
To bring out a buddy,
Bring him out alive.

Friendships born of war
place a mutual trust

Grant Coble

and responsibility on
on one another to bring
each other out.

"Bringing Out a Buddy"
is life itself.

    8/25/1968, William Alan Swoveland, Detroit, Mi, Small Arms Fire, 46W/24
    8/25/1968, Steve Owen Nussbaumer, Hayward, La, Small Arms Fire, 46W/91
    8/26/1968, Again, the next morning, we charged the position, but to our surprise, no one was home. During the night the NVA had pulled out. Finally the call came they had been sighted several clicks away trying to get away. All three troops took chase. Coming upon some valleys, each troop took one as we did not know which the enemy used. B Troop made contact first. I spun around and headed their way. My tank was the first to arrive. They were setting on line, in a rice paddy, firing into a tree line. I decided to pull up on the right flank next to one of B Troop's tanks. Just as we pulled into position a 105 recoilless hit the tank next to us and it exploded. We knocked out the 105. I never knew if any one survived the hit. For an hour we fired upon the tree line. Later we found out several companies were left behind to slow our advance and allow the rest of the NVA Regiment to escape.

    I found out years later we had done battle with 2 NVA Regiments for 4 days. Our unit, the 1/1 Cavalry, received the Presidential Unit Citation for this action. Several months later I found out my friend, Nicky Bacon, had been awarded the Congressional Medal of Honor (CMH). I will always be proud of my service to my country and the fine men I served with. There are no better men in the entire world than these men who fought a thankless war.

    8/28/1968, Charles Don Champion, Irving, TX, Explosive Device, 46W/47
    8/28/1968, Robert C Coonrod, Napa, CA, Explosive Device, 46W/48

8/30/1968, Maurice J Haas, Cassvile, WI, Explosive Device, 45W/06

9/18/1968, Richard Frank Williams, San Leandro, CA, In Captivity, 43E/32

9/24/1968, Mario Pereda Estrada, Inglewood, CA, Small Arms Fire, 42W/04

9/24/1968 HQ, The 1st Squadron 1st Cavalry was in contact with the 2nd BN 1st MF Regiment 3rd NVA Division southwest of Nui Yon (BT2416). The 2nd BN 1st MF Regiment 3rd NVA Division strength at this time was approximately 355. Their mission was to secure the rear elements of the 1st MF Regiment which was withdrawing from the area. The area in which the battle was fought consisted of thickly wooded islands which were surrounded by rice paddies. The enemy was well entrenched in this area and had to be routed out by numerous air strikes. During the operation members of the 2nd BN 1st MF Regiment 2nd NVA Division were captured. The POW's gave the information on their unit and its mission.

11/1968 to 4/1968, Rick Lamison, Captain, Troop Commander

1969

1969, LTC V.C. Cousland, Squadron Commander
1969, LTC R.A. Lawrence, Squadron Commander
1969, LTC Phillip L. Bolte, Squadron Commander

1/23/1969, Gerald Jacob Budbill, Toledo, OH, Accidental Homicide, 34W/64

2/25/1969, James Ellison Scott, Gainesboro, TN, Small Arms Fire, 31W/55

3/11/1969, HQ, C Troop detonated 2 mines and found another mine within 50 meters of the others. There were 4 personnel killed and 3 wounded. The third vehicle in a column detonated the mine. While the injured man was being carried to the dust-off chopper, one of the litter bearers stepped on a mine, killing all three of them and one other man standing nearby. Three more were injured that were standing near the area.

3/11/1969, Perry Leonard Bozeman, Whitmore, CA, Ground Casualty, 29W/04

3/11/1969, Larry Anthony Jackson, New Orleans, LA, Explosive Device, 29W/09

3/11/1969, Paul Wayne Shrewsbury, Newport News, VA, Ground Casualty, 29W/15

3/11/1969, Larry Strahan, Pontiac, MI, Ground Casualty, 29W/15

3/15/1969, William James Hillard II, Kennedy, New York, Explosive Device, 29W/45

4/1969, Ken Yarborough, We were based on Hill 29, Hawk Hill. Sonny, the TC for C-16 got into a conversation with some NVA soldier. The soldier told Sonny he was going to kill him after some insults. Mostly my experiences were good and I met a lot of good people. Day to day life was usually uneventful and rather pleasant. For the most part the war was a good experience. Going through towns and villages, the children would line the streets and we would throw C-rations to them. Young mothers would bring their sick children to Doc and he would do what he could for them. Mostly he would give them a bar of soap which cured most skin disorders.

Tracking around the paddies of South Vietnam is not without it's hazards. One heavily ACAV, full of ammunition, explosives, armed to the teeth, and stuck in the mud.

I enjoyed going to the field, especially as a driver. Going over the berms, I could lower the ACAV down so ever gently. There were some bad times, and when I returned to the states to finish my time in the military, I'd wish I could returned back to Vietnam.

1969, LTC John A. Dure, Squadron commander

4/15/1969, Stephen William Cummings, Holden, MA, Vehicle Crash, 27W/85

5/12/1969, HQ, The Platoons were located at 3 different NDP's. At 0001 Hours C-36 was in a blocking position (vic BT185265) with 1 platoon from the 725th RF Company. This was about 5 clicks SW of Hawk Hill, near the base of a finger protruding from the mountains. C-16 was in a NDP (vic BT210238) just off the Ky My road, route 586, about 5 clicks west of Ky My. C-26 was loggered at Tam Ky as a reaction force.

At 0055 Hours C-16 received 5 mortars and 3 RPG rounds. One PF was dusted off with fragmentation wounds. At 0245 Hours a flare ship and 2 gunships from F Troop 8th Air Cav were on station supporting C-16 due to continued enemy activity.

There was significant other enemy activity happening this might at other locations throughout the 196th Bde's AO. As part of the final phase of the enemy Spring Offensive, VC/NVA forces struck US and ARVN fire bases and installations. Sappers, infiltrating defenses, and hurling satchel charges, attacked LZ Baldy, Center, and Professional, resulting in casualties at all location. These attacks were repulsed with the enemy suffering significant more casualties. During the night Hawk Hill came under sporadic indirect fire and occasional direct small arms fire, but no major sapper attack. However, at the PF outpost Nui Yon, which is located about 10 clicks to the southwest of Tam Ky, the enemy force attacked in strength and quickly over ran the defending PF company. Because this OP dominated major routes of approach to Tam Ky, it had to be recaptured to eliminate the threat of a major enemy attack.

At 0430 Hours the 1/1 Cav TOC received a message from the Division G-3 stating that contact with the advisor at Nui Yon OP was lost at 0200 Hours and apparently the OP was over run by enemy forces. 1/1 Cav was ordered to coordinate with the Arvin's at Tam Ky and prepare to send one platoon along with an element from the 3/4th Cav (ARVN) to retake the outpost at first light. At 0500 Hours C-26, who was located at Tam Ky as reaction force, was given the order to move to the vicinity of Nui Yon and attack at first light. They were delayed until 0655 Hours when they reported on the move.

The first reported contact by C-26 occurred at 0750 Hours at (vic BT250180) when a tank was hit by an RPG round, hitting the tank main gun barrel, resulting in 4 WIA, who were evacuated by dust off. Apparently all hell broke loose for C-26, around 0900 Hours; three tracks were hit by RPGs resulting in the deaths of "Halgrimson, Stegal, and West along with 3 seriously wounded. Kendle was reported as missing. At 2200 Hours one ACAV still remained at (vic BT266182) due to this incident.

5/12/1969, Marloye Keith Halgrimson, Ada, MN, Multiple Fragmentation Wounds, 25W/70

5/12/1969, Randy Truman Kendle, Greencastle, PA, Burns, 25W/76

5/12/1969, Edsel Wayne Steagall, Shady Valley, TN, Multiple Fragmentation Wounds, 25W/86

5/12/1969, Darrell Charles West, Barber Town, Oh, Small Arms Fire, 25W/90

At 0920 Hours B-16 and B-26 were moving from Hawk Hill to assist C-26, and further, at 0930 Hours B-36 was moving to assist C-26. By midday C-36 was also committed in this endeavor to retake the Nui Yon OP. C Troop sustained no further casualties on May 12, however B Troop sustained several WIA during the day.

The VCMF/NVA forces were well dug-in and were able to effectively use mortar fire, RPGs, an heavy automatic weapons fire against the attacking cavalry. During two assaults, the cavalry was met with an intense volume of fire and pulled back as air strikes were processed on the OP. It became apparent that attacks by the cavalry alone were not sufficient to recapture the OP and A, B, and C Companies, 3/21 Infantry were combat air assaulted into the area to reinforce the armored forces. As the 3 infantry companies maneuvered into position during the late afternoon and early evening of 12 May. Further air strikes and artillery fires were placed on the OP.

By evening, with the 3 Companies from the 3/21 Infantry on the battlefield, B Troop returned to Hawk Hill for defense there. A Troop, after being relieved of its part in operation on Barrier Island joined C Troop late that night, in preparation for an attack on 13 May. C-1/1's NDP was at (vic BT208223), in the vicinity of Hill 35. Thus ended the first day of the fight to retake Nui Yon OP.

Cordell Bruce Rogers was killed the next day during the battle to retake Nui Yon OP.

5/13/1969, Cordell Bruce Rogers, Remsen, IA, Wounded, Died 5/27/69, Explosive Device, 23W/01

5/1969 to 9/1969, John R. Estes, Captain, Troop Commander

6/23/1969, Gary Freeman, Norfolk, VA, Vehicle Crash, 22W/118

Grant Coble

6/23/1969, Homer Daniel Thick, Flint, MI, Vehicle Crash, 21W/03

7/21/1969, Raymond Joseph Palandro, Pittsburg, PA, Drowned, 20W/31

7/8/1969, Steve Rockwell, We were just starting to head back north towards Chu Lai after working out south east of LZ Dottie and to the north east of LZ Bronco; or maybe it was Maverick. They turned us around and told us that a grunt unit, the 196th or the 198th, had gotten themselves into an ambush and that we would be saving their OD green butts. The AO (Area of Operation) that we were headed for was south and to the west of LZ Maverick and was called Duc Pho. It ended up being right next to the foot hills and the mountains.

Nothing happened right away. But once we got within about a click of the hills we started receiving small arms fire; but not to bad at first. The weather was hot and dry. I'm driving C-30, Stroud is the TC, we are looking for a way across a trench line that is in the middle of a hedgerow, and find out that it's full of Gooks. Bill asked me very calmly (Not!) to make a hard right an get the track facing the main line of fire. Well when I did that the left track picked that moment to let us know it was time for new track blocks. Needless to say we threw the flipping track off. I remember thinking this can't be good! I wasn't so worried about getting shot so much as what Bill was trying to say to me at that very minute! Well anyway, there we sat taking fire from all around us and that dam track lying on the ground next to us (Bummer!). Bill, I, and one other guy hit the ground, which left two guys manning the M-60's. We knew we had to do something cause things were just getting worse by the minute. Bullets were bouncing off the track every which way. We decided to break and re-mount the track. I remember one time running to the back of the track for something (tools or track blocks) and hearing bullets bouncing off the back ramp. Either they were bad shots or we were very graced, for a lack of a better word.

We finally gave up on trying to get the track back on and another track pulled up, hooked up to us, and pulled us with our track in tow out of the danger area, backwards to our defensive logger. When we got out, we saw our Jerry cans, on the back or the track, looked like Swiss Cheese. Later C-6 would ask Bill how we could throw a track, especially in a fire fight? Gills reply was that he had been trying to get new track blocks for awhile on re-supply as ours were mostly dead. Needless to say we got new track that night on re-supply. You know it's funny, at the time it seemed to take no time for everything to happen, but we managed to go through a whole case of soda before we got back to the logger.

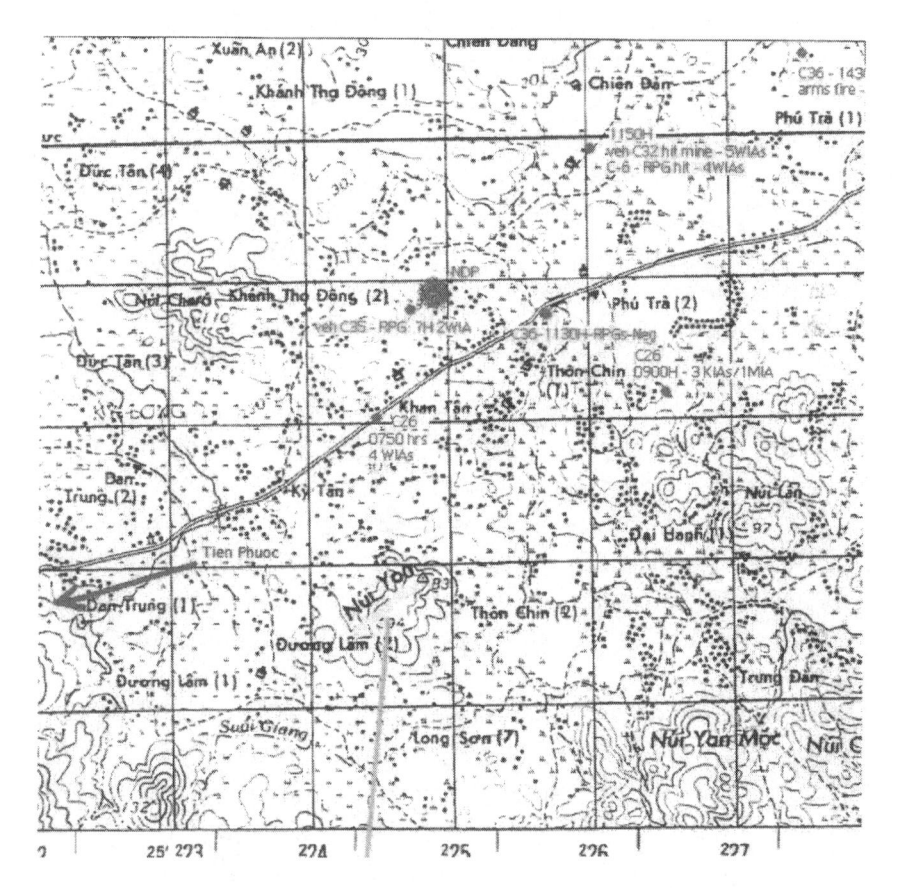

This is a map of the Nui Yon battle field.

Well, that night we replaced our bad track and re-supplied our ammo, water, and what not, and got ready for the next morning. The sun finally rose after a night of loud noise and light sleep. We moved out. When we finally reached the grunts all hell broke lose.

We got between the grunts and the gooks and headed forward.

It's afternoon now. I don't remember exactly how it all came about, but we were on line facing the mountains when all of a sudden off to my right-front, between us and C-34 tank (we had the 48's with us), two dark shadows popped up into the hedgerow in front of us. The next thing I see is a ball of fire headed right for us. I was already moving backward when it hit the right front of the track; smoke, dirt, metal, and all kinds of stuff flew through the air. The impact blew all the inspection panels off inside the track and tossed me up against the side of the drivers compartment, but she kept running long enough for us to back up a ways.

Later they decided that we had taken a RPG-7 and the only thing that saved us was the fact that the engine got in the way and took most of the blast. The whole right side of the engine was gone! How it kept running as long as it did is beyond me, but I've loved Detroit Diesels ever sense. Meanwhile, on the tank next to us, the gunner who went by the name of Rocket, hit the ground and threw a grenade at the spot where the RPG had come from, but it landed short and rolled back under the tank and went off. After that, the TC (Divine), lowered his main gun and put a 90MM in bed with them. I don't know if it worked, but the firing stopped.

Well here we are being towed back into the night logger again. That's twice in two days and what seems the beginning of a bad habit. They sent us back to the rear (LZ Bronco or Maverick) where we spent the rest of the mission and got a new engine pack. We still had the whole from the RPG to show off. It did get a lot of looks (like from the VN 3/4 Cavalry). The worst thing of the whole mission was that we had finally gotten our transmission to shift into hi gear on the road march down and had done pretty good against the other tracks on the beach racing (Me Lai Summer Nationals). Oh well, it was just the beginning of a month to remember.

8/11/1969, Ken Yarborough, The tanks have left for Chu Lai and the rest of the unit is to follow. There are many vacant guard bunkers. During the night one manned guard bunker from either 2nd or 3rd Platoon fires on some VC in the rice paddy while using a starlight scope. We in 1st Platoon didn't hear anything about it until later in our bunker. Most of us were still awake when we began to hear explosions, gun fire, and sporadic gun fire. Our bunker seemed to be the only one not on fire. Someone opened up on a line of soldiers running past the mess hall without any apparent results. SGT Mike Cloward and I sat hunched down pondering what to do as only a few M-16's were among us. Cloward asked me if I was ready to make a break for one of the tracks? It seemed the right thing to do rather than being without a rifle. "I'm not sure. There's an awful lot of lead flying around." We made a break for it and arrived at C-17. The SGT mounted the cupola and the 50 and I the driver's seat. We headed over to C-18 and began firing outside the perimeter. I got back onto one of the 60's. There was fighting all over the hill. As it turned out most of the battle was in the C Troop AO.

The battle seemed to be fairly short. There were many casualties on both sides. Many of us thought we were being overran by a large enemy force but ended up being a well manned sapper unit. They came through the wire at a vacant guard position and attacked manned tracks with grenades and RPG's. One Trooper named Jody attempted to pick one grenade up from the floor of his track and throw it back when it blew his hand off. I think he died from his wounds.

After the chaos died down we began to load up some of the wounded and take them to HQ for med-avac. One guy we thought of as old because he had 6 days left before going home died in the back of the track. He'd been sleeping on top of a bunker occupied by several crews including C-1-6 along with 5 others. A grenade went off among them.

Grant Coble

ACAV equipped with flame thrower. Notice the crew has no shields for gunners. The track was not taken into the field very often and some considered it a liability due to it's explosive nature if hit by a RPG or mine.

ACAV's would break down while on a mission, or hit a mine, requiring repairs in the field as this crew is conducting here. Over the 60 shields are bandoleers of clips for M16 rifles. Each crew would set up their track to suit them in every day life and battle.

Another named Finnigan, who we called Finny, was also injured. After arriving at HQ, he opened his eyes and asked me if they were still there. I told him "yes" but there was a lot of blood. I lied. The concussion had blown them out. Pete also couldn't see. One fellow we called Top was killed in the beginning when he went to the outhouse. Upon exiting he was shot in the back by a sapper. C-1-6 was killed when he ran out to man a 50. The guard must have already been killed. C-1-6 was standing using a 60 when an RPG hit the track.

There were a lot of bloody cots at HQ and all were filled. There were several Chu Hois also. One was in real bad shape and I held the IV bottle for him. One guy walked by and said "just let him die." He did. We were up all the rest of the night. At dawn what was left of us surveyed the damage. Most of the C Troops bunkers had been destroyed. There were a lot of dead sappers lying around. Some guy had shot one point blank in the head. Another chased one down and killed him with his M-16 after a grenade was thrown into his bunker

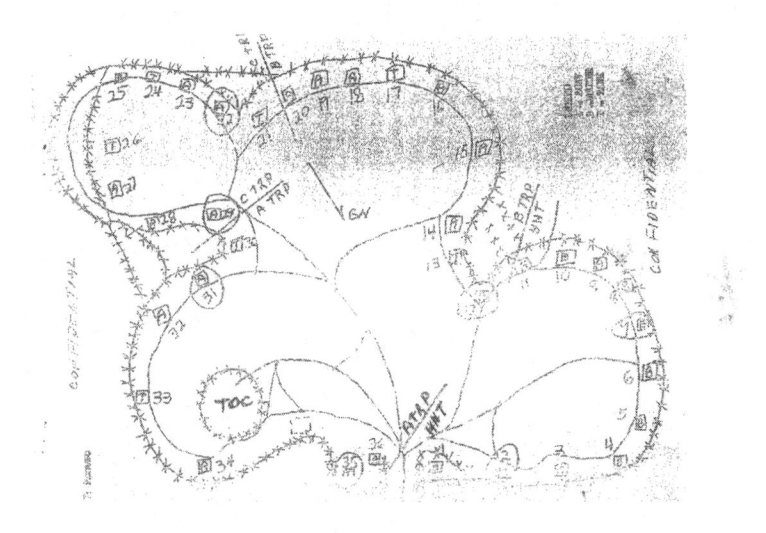

This drawing shows the layout for the defense of Hawk Hill. The lines with "X" spaced on them indicate concertina wire. The squares with letters followed by numbers indicate which track will be assigned to that location. TOC is radio communications center. Each Troop had its own area of responsibility. During the sapper attack in 1969 C Troop was caught in the middle of moving to Chu Lia and thus had holes in the defense of the hill.

Grant Coble

8/12/1969, James Anthony Cabral Jr, Cambridge, MA, Burns, 19W/10

8/12/1969, Eugene Paul Clark, Albemarie, NC, Rocket, 19W/11

8/12/1969, Donald Gary Dillard, Wapato, WA, Multiple Fragmentation Wounds, 19W/12

8/12/1969, Lawrence Day Greef, Portland, OR, Multiple Fragmentation Wounds, 19W/13

8/12/1969, James Linder Jr, Miami, FL, Multiple Fragmentation Wounds, 19W/17

8/12/1969, David Oscar Haake, Nashville, IL, Rocket, 19W/14

8/12/1969, James Larry Johnson, Eldridge, AL, Rocket, 19W/16

8/12/1969, Bradley Joseph Simmons, Ancramdale, NY, Explosive Device, 19W/23

We had a meeting in the mess hall that morning. The number was in the teens present.

The dead sappers were loaded up in duce-and-a-half and hauled to the local village and dumped. At least 2 loads went.

Replacements began to show up that afternoon. You can only imagine the look in their eye's when they walked into the AO.

During one patrol southwest of Tam Ky we came to a small village with some straw hooch's. A dismount was ordered. The 60 gunner had a bad feeling and didn't want to go and as I'd been driving all morning I volunteered. As I approached a thick hedge row I noticed a part of it had been cut away as if to make a path. I inserted the barrel of my M-16 in and separated what was left of vegetation. In front, past a ditch, were 3 NVA soldiers. One had an RPG, the other an AK-47, and the third was pulling the string on a Chicom grenade. I yelled, "Dinks, Dinks" at the 4 or 5 guys behind me and began to run, firing over my soldier as I went. The grenade landed behind the ditch and blew up. The RPG went over my head and missed the track. The 3 ran past the other side of the hedgerow and into 2nd Platoon, who killed one and captured the other two.

On another mission west of Hawk Hill, we left 2 tracks at an ARVN outpost that had been coming under constant attack at night.

The rest of us moved out to a NDP (night defensive position) and were getting settled down for the night when a call came in that the hill was under attack. We moved out to the location using star clusters to eliminate our way. When we arrived we found the Arvin's had taken heavy casualties.

On a mission, I think west of Duc Pho, a company of infantry came under heavy contact. We were called for support. 1st Platoon arrived first and one of the tanks took a RPG with but no casualties.. The driver began backing up when he was shot through the mouth. The bullet went in one cheek and out the other. Keeping calm, he continued backing out of the area. Shortly we were all engaged with the enemy. The battle started in the morning and raged all day.

NDP (night defensive position). Arvin's dug in while ACAV crews generally slept on or near their tracks. Fox holes for the crew were an option most of the time. Breakfast was the first order of the day.

I pulled up beside 2 grunts on the ground manning a 60. Both were injured but continued the fight. Laying down a good field of fire allowed both to get behind the ACAV for medical treatment and a dust off. One was from our medic's home town. He thought they'd both live. The infantry had a lot of casualties.

Tank retrievers and their crews sometimes have it tough. A mine took the idler off this machine and they had to be towed home.

My TC told me to keep my head down so I wouldn't get hit. This was very nerve racking not being able to see anything. So, I raised my seat and entered the fray with my M16 spraying anything and everything. I continued this until dark approached and we pulled back.

We worked late that night restocking our tracks with ammo. When morning came we again approached the fire fight but met only sporadic fire. The infantry began taking a body count that went over 500 enemy dead.

One night as we pulled into our NDP, I had an uneasy feeling. There was a berm about the height of our track and I pulled behind it. I was setting in the TC's hatch during my guard, late at night, when an RPG hit in front of me. Every one opened up with their 50's for some time. We didn't really want anyone shooting at us again that night. The next morning I checked out where the RPG landed and found it hit 2 foot below the top of the berm and directly in front of me. My lucky day.

We were west of Tam Ky one day and getting ready to negotiate a steep steam crossing when one of the tracks hit a mine blowing off its track and idler. A decision was made to call for a tank retriever and haul the ACAV back. Upon arrival and getting into position to hook up to the ACAV, the tank retriever also hit a mine, blowing off his idler and track. Another retriever came and fetched them both. We did a mine sweep and found one other mine, blowing it in place. We were very nervous and careful to stay on our tracks. We were very happy to line up and leave this place.

A while later, as we traveled along, the 7th track in our convoy hit a mine, sending it and its crew up into the air. I remember seeing crew members doing summer-salts above the dust. The track landed upside down, but at least the crew was alive, but hurt. The driver was still in his seat. I looked underneath and saw the driver reaching out for help in getting out. Later they all returned to duty. It was decided to blow the track in place. We returned to Hawk Hill without further incident.

Stream crossing's can be very interesting and dangerous. With a full load of ammunition, an ACAV can swim with about 6 inches to spare. It does help if there are no RPG holes in the sides. A bilge pump helps keep the track dry if a leak does appear.

Grant Coble

Anthony John Newman, "Charlie One-Nine,"
Land mines abound,
Placed underground,
Just like the one,
Charlie one-nine found.

A two-five-zero pounder,
Laced with napalm,
Burned several hours,
Till all but shell was gone.

Arkie and George,
Frenchie and Jim,
Each of them paid,
On this VC's whim.

Hurtled in the air,
This Tinkertoy tank,
Only the builders of Sheridans,
Of which to thank.

Its own rounds exploding,
To add to the fare,
Torn apart internally,
All but one life to spare.

Jim blown out again,
On his first mission back,
George burnt to the third degree,
While driving this track.

They said Arkie's wounds,
Would heal just fine,
Poor Frenchie lost,
In the battle for time.

Where is the Limey,
In this time of gloom?
When those on his track,
Suffered this doom.

Coming out to the field,
On a chopper festooned,
With a couple of newbees,
For Charlie to wound.

Pictorial memory,
I have etched in my mind,
Of returning to the field,
And my comrades not to find.

To make it through this,
I knew that I would,
But to eliminate the memories,
God, I wish that I could.

    I was returning to Hawk Hill from a 3 day in country R&R by Huey chopper along with 4 or 5 other fellow troopers. We were very high and just cruising along, I loved flying in choppers, when all of a sudden we started dropping like a rock dropped over a cliff. I looked at the guys sitting next to me and their eyes were as big as saucers, as I'm sure mine were. The pilot looked around at us and smiled, then calmly flipped the master switch back on. We were all sure our day had come, and the pilot had a good laugh.

    9/1/1969, Department of The Army, From the Commanding General of Americal Division to HQ, 1st Squadron, 1st Regiment of Dragoons; 1 - In the past armored cavalry units normally moved through the middle of rice paddies in column formation. We believed that this was the best tactic to use in order to minimize mine casualties. However, experience has shown that many times mines will detonate after several ACAVs have passed over it, thereby demonstrating the ineffectiveness of the tactic. 2 - In order to reestablish relative freedom of movement for the ACAVs, it was necessary to become unpredictable in our movement techniques. That is to say that on some occasions the Troops and Platoons will move on line and sometimes they will move in column. We no longer go through the middle of the rice paddies as a regular practice. Sometimes the units will travel on the edge of the paddies and sometimes they will travel through the center of the paddies. The important point is that we try to move by using unpredictable techniques. 3 - Operation: Defense of Fire Base against rocket attack. A. Two "rocket watch" guard posts have been established. Both posts are located so that the guards will have excellent views of the general area from which the rockets have been launched. B. Selected personnel have been trained in map reading and azimuth shooting. Those people and the artillery forward observer teams are used to man these posts during early morning and late evening hours. If they sight any rocket firings they immediately shoot an azimuth on the firing sight and report the azimuth to the artillery. The artillery then triangulates to determine the location of the firing positions an commences counter-battery fire. C. As a deterrent to emplacement and firing of rockets this unit uses the Aero Scouts to conduct visual reconnaissance of our "rocket pocket." The VR is accomplished right after first light in the morning and just prior to last light at night (It is too early for us to evaluate the effectiveness of these measures due to the general lull in activity). 4. Operations: Defense of Fire Base. A. This unit has experienced some difficulty in the area of employment of the clamor mine in defense of the perimeter. Specifically the problem is that the mines are not properly sighted to get the desired coverage of the perimeter when they are employed each night. B. In order to eliminate the problems a competent NCO was shown precisely where each mine should be emplaced and what area it should cover. The NCO then cemented the mine mounts into the ground. This results in a permanent installation and ensures proper coverage. With the mines employed in depth and providing complete coverage of an area it is of little consequence that VC/NVA reconnaissance would be able to locate the mines. 5. Operations: Defense of fire Base. a. We have experienced some difficulty in placing fire on targets detected by the use of the star light scopes. Many times the man with the star light scope can not explain to a gunner where the fire should be placed. b. To alleviate the above situation the star light scopes are being mounted on the M-16 rifles are bore-sighted. The men using the star lights scope can then fire on a target he detects using tracer ammunition. This will then identify the target for other gunners. 6. Emphasis has been placed on the use of artillery as the most responsive means to reinforce and/or support ground maneuvers. In the past it has been habitual to call for gunship support first which negates the use of artillery. The combination of both air and artillery fire is preferable and possible if artillery is called first.

9/1969 To 4/1970, David Miller, Captain, Troop Commander

9/1969, David Miller, To begin this story we need some background. I had completed a tour with E Troop of the 11th Brigade and A Troop, 1/1 Cavalry in 1967 to 1968. I was stationed at Fort Knox as the Brigade Maintenance Officer for the Training Brigade after that tour. I had asked to be assigned to a company so I could get some command time. I was continually told, "as soon as a replacement became available for me in the Major/Ordnance slot I'd be moved." Through some digging, I found a replacement had never been requested. What's more, the CO liked my work and was not willing to give me up. That OMO School left a mark on my record I couldn't hide. During an Armor Branch visit from D.C., then LTC Graves, informed me it was a raw deal for sure, but there was nothing they could do. I could however request a transfer to Vietnam which couldn't be refused. I had only been home 6 months. I said I'd do it. The Colonel told me to start the paperwork on my end and he'd start everything going on his end. The outcome was, I got my orders before the Brigade Commander ever signed my request. The orders included a statement that I was a second tour volunteer for Vietnam with a stipulation I should be sent to the unit of my choice, 1/1 Cavalry.

Nine months after I left Vietnam I returned to Cam Rah Bay. The statement in my orders saved the day. Infantry Captains in the Repot Depot who had volunteered for specific units surrounded me. The Absence of a similar statement in their orders put them at the mercy of the Repot Depot personnel. Few got their wishes granted.

I got as far as the Americal Division with the statement of 1/1 Cav placement. There I ran into another roadblock. I was informed the Cav had excess officers. My orders were cut to a Grunt Recon unit out in the mountains unless I could convince the Cav to take me and carry me as excess. I begged a jeep off one of the cadre at the week long jungle warfare indoctrination school and got to the Cav. The cadre NCO had been in my platoon during my first tour in A Troop. I drove down to the Cav HQ. The XO was the only one around but was willing to give an old Cavalry Trooper a break.

A few days later I arrived at the Cav to meet an unnamed colonel in charge. He asked me what I wanted to do. I told him I volunteered for one reason, to get combat command time. I was informed that being a reserve officer on active duty, that wasn't going to happen. He saved his command slots for "Regular Army Officers," not part time soldiers. No amount of discussion could change that. I would be Assistant S-1 until some other rear area job came up for a Captain.

I trudged and grumbled along for a couple weeks in that spot. One day I got a call to report to the CO. In the outer office I was met by a smiling XO who informed me I was going to be told by the colonel that he had reconsidered and was going to try me as CO of C Troop. The facts, as related to me by the XO, were that the CO of the troop had been wounded and the job was given to the S1, who promptly refused. Seems the West Point grad had less than four months left in country and was getting out of the Army as soon as he could in one piece. He wanted nothing to do with a field assignment. I played along, thanked him profusely for his vote of confidence, and assured him I would not let him down.

9/13/1969, Grant Coble, 9/10/1969 to 9/11/1970, I arrived in Cam Rah Bay and was transferred to Chu Lai. My first night I pull guard in a bunker alongside a dirt road by the China Sea. We had one rifle with one clip between the 4 of us. 13,000 miles from home, scared shitless, stories that spooked us even more, and little protection. "Wonderful!" During my turn at guard, late at night, a jeep pulls up and some dude wants passage. I stood in the road blocking them with the rifle in plain view. I informed them they could not pass without either the proper markings on the bumper or written permission. They had neither. The passenger jumps back into the jeep and orders the driver to advance. Well, I locked and loaded the rifle and brought it to a position that got the drivers attention. He jumped on the brakes. I repeated myself again and I think they believed me as a quick retreat was taken. Wheather I would have shot something was for sure, but what?

Anthony John Newman, "In Country",
Eighteen hours,
To do nothing but sit,
Trying to make reason,
Scared enough to shit.

Tarmac glistens, an ocean of heat,
Vents rush in hot air, I sweat in my seat,
Realizing any second could be my last,
Surrealistically running through events in my past.

Stewardesses look at us as though we have died,
None of them look at us with a semblance of pride.
With murmured soft talking, we exit the plane,
Each asking individually, Is this really sane?

A line of short-timers walk the other way,
Each smiling, not laughing, this is their day.
I reach out and touch one, for words he might say,
He solemnly, with distant voice said, "C-Y-A."

9/16/1969, Eliseo Vergara, Anton, TX, Explosive Device, 18W/98

9/23/1969, Grant Coble, The Troop had only been back a day or two when I arrived. Seems they just came back from a rather nasty fire fight and were still talking about it. 3 days from my arrival we were on our way again near the area they last went. It was monsoon season and I would not be dry again for weeks. We headed for the LZ English area south and west of Chu Lai. I was the 5th man on an ACAV, the Platoon Sergeant's track. SGT Chastine, Jone's driving,

Lumley the left gunner, and Dunlap the right gunner, and me in the middle.

We crossed paddy after paddy, getting stuck, get pulled out, and get stuck again. Sometimes one would wade in water 2 to 3 feet deep; alive with critter life. Just knew one would attack me and drag me away to a horrible death. "What the hell am I doing here?" Always wet and covered in mud: No escape from the constant rain, and cold.

One day we went up to LZ English for what turned out to be a short visit. Seems someone pissed someone off and we had to leave. We ended up in a paddy, at least higher as the water did drain to lower locations, for some well deserved hot chow flown in. We were enjoying the meal when loud, angrily bee sounds surrounded us. Then the loud "Boom Boom Boom" sound of artillery hitting just in front of us sent all into hiding. Well, I guess we "really must have pissed someone off" for a grunt company sneaked up on us but did not know what we were. They opened up and call in support on some noises located on the other side of the woods. Lousy shots they were. Captain Miller informed us what had just happened and not to shoot anyone we saw going over a certain hill to our northeast. It was kind of funny to see a company of grunts hauling ass single file.

This mission was my first experience with a Mad Minute. This entailed the use of all weapons at a prescribed time and area, generally after nightfall. Well, I dismounted and located myself beside the ACAV with my trusty M-16, ready to rock and roll. I squatted and was ready. The roar was overwhelming and the sight of a wall of moving red (every fifth round is a tracer) was breathtaking. Of course I watched this from a sitting position not so much from the almost non-existent recoil of the M-16, as the stunning shock to what I was witnessing and hearing. Sitting in 6 inches of water never even crossed my mind until after several moments passed.

9/29/1969, Jimmy Kuhlenhoelter, Boeling Green, KY, Multiple Fragmentation Wounds, 17W/18

10/1969, Carl Wronko, Next Stop, Fort Knox, Kentucky. Home of the Armor Branch. My Orders tell me that I will be assigned here permanent duty on completion of my training. This time living is better. I am given my very own apartment which I share with a Signal Officer Lt. By the fall of 1969, I am finished with Armor Officer Basic and become a Training Officer in the Training Brigade, where we train draftees in the art of caring for and fighting in a tank or an M-113. Actually, the NCO's do the training: I just stand around and make a presence, which is fine because I am usually nursing a hangover from my nightly trip down to Louisville, Ky. Then my luck turns good again. My skills are recognized! I happen to sit next to a Major at the Officer's Club one evening while we both are in civilian clothing. We get along fine. He asks where I am assigned and then offers me a job working for him. He is the Commanding General's aide and I can join him as an Assistant General's Aide. To my question about what I would be doing, he replies that I will be giving tours of Fort Knox to visitors, including ROTC Cadets and Army Vets of World War 2 and Korea.

So, I put on the General's Aid arm patch and begin giving tours: and, keep going to Louisville every night. Life is good. I'm glad I joined the Army. I also find out that no Second Lt. from Ft. Knox had been sent to Vietnam in a year. The Major tells me he has my permanent change of duty orders being worked on and I should get them shortly. I get a call from my old training Brigade unit that my Orders are in so over I go to receive them. When the Captain hands them to me he has a big grin on his face. Why, I ask myself, as he didn't like it when I got taken from him and posted to the General's Staff. I started to read. Not going to the General's Staff after all. I read that I am to go to the Panama Canal Zone to Fort Sherman for jungle training: and then I am assigned to USARV or United States Army Republic of Vietnam. Seems when Nixon invaded Cambodia that the 11th Armored Cav lost a whole lot of platoon leaders and they had caught me up in an emergency draft. Off I go, with the distinction of being the one and only Armor Second Lt. to go from Ft. Knox in a year. My what a privilege.

When I get to the Canal Zone, I have the pleasure of meeting up with many of my classmates from my old OCS Infantry Company. While I enjoy the event, I begin to realize that when the Army put me in the Armor Branch they retained my Infantry Officer's MOS as well. Shit happiness, I am going to go through the Infantry Jungle

School with my Infantry Classmates. I am going to be a Tanker trained in jungle fighting. If I can only figure how to get the tanks into the jungle, why do I feel that I'm destined to go back to the Infantry. My Classmates welcome me back with big smiles. I don't reciprocate. We are also told at the Jungle School that if we travel directly to our duty station in Vietnam, the two weeks of schooling will count toward our fifty-two weeks in Vietnam. Lovely, guess who has already put in for more leave after Jungle School? I am awarded my diploma as a jungle expert. My mother would be so proud.

Well, now I am a very well trained Armor/Infantry/Jungle Expert with two weeks leave.

11/1969, Grant Coble, An IG Inspection was due and Top is sending every man to the field he can. I ended up the 5th man on a motor track. It was still monsoon season and really tough to find a place to sleep on a motor track much less being the 5th man. After 3 days someone must have felt sorry for me and I was sent back.

The day of the inspection, what was left of our platoon loaded up on 4 ACAV's and left for the day. Our first stop was the dump. The flies were terrible and a hasty retreat was ordered. "But where now?" Someone came up with the idea to go to Tam Ky. The only question was how to get past the guards. This was solved by approaching the gate at a rather high speed and the lead track TC frantically waving his arms. It worked and off we went.

Our first stop was at a whore house just north of Tiem Phouc road. The second track didn't have brakes and only by sheer driving skill did the driver avoid a terrible wreck. Once he backed up what seemed a quarter mile, he verbally unloaded on the lead track TC. However, once he paid his respects to the house owner and met his daughter, he felt much better.

We continued on into Tam Ky and crossed the new wooden bridge that replaced the old, blown, concrete bridge. The old bridge was up river from the new one and we stopped at its old approach, dismounted, and went out onto the bridge with grenades in hand. Our first volley was quite a sight going off under water. Kind of like depth charges going off,: boiling and foaming water with little water spouts. We were about to toss another round when the old bridge began swaying violently side to side. We stood crouched knowing that each sway would be our last and tumbled into the river, but it did stop. The sound of splashes down stream caught our attention. There must have been 3 dozen ARVN soldiers swimming in uniform and many wore steel pots, carrying sand bags and scooping up the hundreds of dead or dying fish. They kept yelling, "More grenades!" I remember one fellow falling the 20 foot drop with a full sand bag and his knife stuck in it. I never did see him surface and we never did toss any more grenades from the old concrete bridge again.

Once, during my visit to South East Asia, did we have a stand down that included a steak meal, on the beach, in the resort town "Chu Lia." It was a beautiful day; hot, sunny, warm water, sandy beach, and peaceful. About the only thing missing were the beautiful bathing beauties in their "Then" skimpy two piece bathing suites. We had to settle for........., well, don't ask!

We body surfed, played ball, snoozed, drank well, ate well, built sand castles, and just plain enjoyed the day. The one thing I remember most about the day was a damaged toe nail being ripped off by the waves. I expected pain and was relieved at its absence, and thrilled with having left part of me in the sea. Hopefully that's all I left behind.

1969, LTC Richard Graves, Squadron Commander

12/13/1969, David Miller, We were working on the Batanga Peninsula, OPCON to the 198th. We had been there for a couple weeks as I recall. Well, the Infantry Brigade commander and I had had a couple of heated discussions over the two weeks as to the best way to use our troop and how we weren't getting properly re-supplied etc. We really didn't like each other very much.

On the morning of the 13th, a Blues element of SRX people had been inserted to investigate a pack laying on the ground. The problem was they were inserted into the middle of an NVA sapper unit. I had said I could reach the surrounded ground unit but was told to stay off the radio as the Infantry would be inserted and take care of it. The grunts wanted their action and weren't willing to let the Cavalry play in their war. We were about five clicks away. I convinced the Air Cav to give me a LOH to fly over the area as the troop moved. They dropped me back at my track when we were within a click of the action. The grunts never could get choppers to insert some infantry.

We had a little firefight going on to rescue the Blues that had been inserted into the middle of the NVA. Things were getting under control when my radio crackled on the troop net and a Charlie Charlie bird circled overhead. I was told to pop smoke to receive a bird. Someone up above wanted to come down and mess with me I figured. I told them, it was a hot area, we were under fire and it wasn't safe. Again, I was told to pop smoke, that he wanted to come down. I believe my words were something along the line of, "It's not safe to land, I'm taking fire from front and rear. I don't have time to entertain. Stay off my damn troop radio. I've got things to do!!!" There was so ever a brief pause and the voice came back with something along the lines of, "I didn't ask if it was safe. I'm coming in, so pop the smoke. I want to land on the right side of the war!!!"

Reluctantly, I popped smoke as the bird banked sharply and hurled towards us. The bird landed and out jumps this almost familiar smallish figure. He quickly hustles to my track and climbs over the back. It was none other than our NEW squadron commander, LTC Graves. I about dropped my teeth when he told me who he was. Then I realized he was responsible for me being where I was, back in the Cav. Here all the time I thought it was some grunt wannabe and it was the same man that a few months earlier had hustled through my orders to get me back to the 1/1 Cav. I didn't know we were getting a new Squadron CO. I'd been out of touch for a couple weeks working OPCON far from home. For the next hour or two he rode around on the back of the track, not saying much, not giving orders, just taking it all in. We said our good-byes a couple hours later with his parting words, "I'll get you back to the Cav as soon as I can". Because it was near the site of the My Lia incident of a year earlier we had to secure the bodies for the night so VIP's could come in and count them the next day. But that's another story with some humor in it the Colonel reminded me of 30 years later.

A couple days later our tour with the Brigade was terminated with one final parting argument over tactics. The Brigade Commander told me to NEVER come back to his AO. I called LTC Graves and told him I was in trouble with the Grunts. He told me not to worry and come on home. After all, we killed 53 NVA, captured 11, destroyed well fortified bunkers, all in 5 hours, and with only 3 wounded.

He never mentioned the smoke-popping incident as long as we were there. He did however bring up my indiscretion, and a couple others, to my wife some 30 years later when we met again. We all had a good laugh over dinner with a twinkle in our eyes for when we met again. The Army in their wisdom got it right as evidenced by his promotions and career assignments. Now we're proud to just call him "The General," our leader.

Dave Miller received 2 Purple Hearts, 1 Bronze Star, 1 Silver Star, 1 Army Commendation Medal, Vietnamese Cross of Gallantry, and the Combat Infantry Badge during two tours in Vietnam

12/20/1969, Grant Coble, Christmas was only a few days away and we were at base camp for the holidays. Bob Hope was in town giving a USO show and we were invited. Mike Kelly was on the duce-and-a-half and I was about to climb on when Sgt. Chastine came up telling me we had a mission. "No way in Hell" was my response to this and his was "Damn sure is, now get the rest of the crew. We're going to LZ Gator for the Holidays." The language I used at this time I will omit. I told Mike, found Emory Williams, and we packed up and moved out with the M-48 and one from 1st Platoon to Gator. Goes without saying we were really pissed off! That is, except for Chastine. I think he liked it.

Upon arriving at Gator, we were shown our areas of assignment. Tank positions dozed out within the wire at so called strategic locations. Personally, I thought the location sucked. Good avenues of approach on either side of us with no clear line of fire at either. But hey, what do I know. As it was the end of the Monsoon season, we still needed someway of staying out of the rain so off we went reconnoitering pallets and ponchos as floors and tent. Within the day we had a nice set-up, dry and somewhat clean. Never did meet the dozen grunts from the base camp missing ponchos.

A guard tower stood out in front of us which restricted our firing points during peaceful time, but would be "no problem" should we have guest. The grunts pulled guard in some sand bagged bunkers between each tower. A road ran all the way around the hill and

Grant Coble

at night a jeep came around with coffee and cake. This wasn't so bad. We were informed that intelligence said the hill was to be hit sometime during Christmas or New Years and that was why we were there. As the gunner, I began by locating all features in my field of fire, tube elevation for each, and round selection for each feature. With these written down I began the everyday life of one bored person stuck on this hill.

For fun we spent the day shooting our M-16's at what ever tripped our triggers, slept, or wondered off exploring what little Gator had to offer. We took turns going for hot chow at the Grunts mess hall. Their cooks lacked the skills of our cooks so eating C-rations was an option.

At night, once we were given the all clear, we began shooting at certain targets with the main gun, blowing the hell out of everything. If Chuck was going to pay a visit, he had to pay his dues first. As we slept most of the day, we stayed up most of the night banging away. I don't think the grunt guards appreciated this as they couldn't sleep either with all the noise. Sometimes we would let a few rounds off parallel to the hill. The percussion alone would knock anyone off their feet outside the tank and down range, where one grunt bunker was located. I can only imagine what was going through their minds. We blew the dickens out of an Island that night. Next morning we viewed the damage, which looked more like the beach landing at "Tarara" during WW-2. Maybe a few trees still stood.

Our only problem came in the disguise of a Sergeant Major. It seemed the grunts, when ever they left their hooch, had to wear steel pots, flack jackets, and carry their M-16's. Now, for a bunch of tankers, used to wearing a pair of shorts and sandals in a secured area, this was a surprise. However, surprise quickly turned to out right war as we were told we were expected to wear the same attire during our visits in their AO. Thus, WW-3. Even Chastine thought this was too much. Well, here comes the SGT Major and he and Chastine lock horns, nose to nose, swapping insults, raising arms in provocative jesters, circling each other, until Chastine motions for us to break camp. This got the SGT Major's attention as we dismantled our AO and prepared to move out. He said something to the nature, "You can't do that" and Chastine's "Watch us!" led to a quick resolution. Helmet liners and a weapon of our choice was the dress code after that when going for chow.

Now, Chastine liked his vodka. He had a couple of 5th's with him and plenty of tomato juice. While we blew the hell out of everything, he drank. One night he decided to retire to the top of the guard tower some 50 feet in front and 20 feet to the left of our position. I had the location greased in as not to hit the tower. Well, I guess after many nights of shooting the main gun, the tower had had enough and collapsed, with Chastine still inside. Emory Williams screams to cease fire puzzled me. Popping up through the hatch, I was greeted with a very unusual sight, yet maybe not as the guys were searching for Chastine buried in the rubble. As the tower was some 50 foot in the air and the sides had collapsed, both outward and inward, the sandbags, used to insulate the occupants, were now laying where they fell, Chastine was still to be located. Joining the search and rescue was the easy part. Finding Chastine was a different matter. Well, we did find him and he was fine. Being he passed out he never knew what happened, and when he did come to, laughed, and took another hit off the unbroken bottle, and passed out again.

New Years night was a sight to see. Everyplace one looked, you saw star clusters and flares illuminating the sky. Tracers added to the wonderful sight. This was also our last night stuck on this pile of dirt and rock. We packed up and dede'd the AO with out so much as a thank you. Two nights later they got hit.

1970

1/1970, Grant Coble, The first week of January the word came down that the Army was taking away our M-48's and M-60's and giving us some new fangled tank called a Sheridan. Only a few guys had been trained on them or seen them. We didn't like the idea for what we had heard wasn't real assuring.

We went out to the field and I pulled my last mission on an ACAV. As I wasn't real fond of them and when getting back in, 9 brand new Sheridans sat waiting for us, I was ready to try them out. We went through some basic training for one day and night. Shooting, driving, and maintenance. Not everyone liked the new tracks. I didn't like the idea we had to guess the range to a target but the track system was very impressive. Al most impossible to throw a track. I saw it happen only once. And very little upkeep. The 152 MM cannon had a very nasty bite compared to the M-48's and M-60's, but not the range.

We were given an old fuel tanker to practice on. All 9 of us were lined up and ready. Once the order is given to fire, you count 1001,1002 an fire. This gives the loader time to be clear of the recoil. I did as trained. Well, not all did, as was evident. The sight through the sights were awesome! The trailer disappeared in a huge cloud of smoke and reappeared in flight, tumbling, twisting, and turning in mid-air. For us that didn't fire, our turn came when the trailer hit the ground. Very little was left to recognize it as a trailer when the firing ceased.

During the practice, Danny Harger, who sported one very cool, well waxed, handle bar mustache, about 1.5 inches long, popped up out of the loaders hatch for some fresh air. There stood a Sergeant Major staring at him. The next words out of his mouth sent a chill down Danny's back, "Cut it now!"

3/1970, We were working the Pineapple Forest country looking for any kind of trouble we could find. One village lay at the base of a very rocky ridge. A nice place to live back home. One woman was present with 4 children and a NVA pith helmet on the ground. Definitely a reason to suspect someone else was present, but where?

We took each kid behind a hooch and shot a 45 cal round into the ground trying to make the mother think we had executed her child. We didn't. This was done 3 times with no results for she never talked. She screamed with horror and cried something terrible. I never, ever, involved myself with anything like that again. I felt terrible and very ashamed for what we put her through. War maybe for keeps, but this was too much. I can only hope, somehow, she forgave us for that day. If I could go back and find her, I would apologize for our action. I've lived with that guilt all my life.

We followed up with a ground search of the area which led us to climb to the ridge line. The face of the cliff was a perfect place for someone to hide. Between the giant boulders that made up the face were dark, forbidding spaces, men could easily hide. Not one of us dared enter any of these spaces; not because the enemy might be present, but snakes. The view from the top was great. One could see all over the place. I think when we realize just how far from the unit we had ventured, we lost some sense of security and quickly returned to our fellow comrades and our tracks. So much for the "tough" American Soldier.

Another village we entered had no one present. It was well used with well worn paths and well cultivated fields with some type of crop. A ground search revealed nothing. One out building, made of straw and mud with a straw roof, had a sheet metal door, secured with two wires. I began to reach to undo the wires, but stopped short. Great booby trap! For the next few minutes I busied myself punching a hole into the side of the building large enough to accommodate a grenade. About the time I completed this project, the Lt. ordered us to mount up. Now, not wanting this work to go to waste, I pulled the pin and inserted the grenade and ran like hell followed by a dive to the ground. "Bang!" A quick look backwards revealed the metal door skipping across the ground, missing me by what seemed inches, at a very high velocity. It seems there was a larger charge other than my grenade. I think I might have pissed the Lt. off as I didn't yell "Fire in the hole." It was fine with me as I was still alive, maybe lighter, but alive. I nimbly went back to the track and sat quietly, still shaking inside. I finished scraping my leg in private later.

Grant Coble

4/1970 to 10/1970, John LaRoche, Captain, Troop Commander

4/2/1970, During the spring we spent most of our time working from Hawk Hill. We had been given Sheridans to replace the 48's and 60's and had been crossed trained on them. At first we did not like the tracks, but as time passed we began to appreciate the change. They were fast, mobile, light, and next to impossible to throw a track. The only thing we didn't like was the aiming system. You had to guess the range when shooting a HE or Black Death round. Canisters, you just aimed in the general direction you wanted the round to go and fire, with devastating effect.

Well, here we were, in or near the Pineapple Forest on a mission to change batteries for a ground sensor device. In flies these 2 officers, we move to another location, and they dismount. The area was brush covered knolls with rice paddies in the low spots. On a "very" big hill, with a sheer cliff facing us, was a lone hooch. I always wished I'd taken a picture of this but didn't.

The officers and Dale Gronsky dismount and begin to wonder into the brush when I hear Dale yell. Turning, he is standing there, bare chest, holding his Thompson Sub Machine gun over his head, laughing and smiling his usual smile, and having a good time. He wanted to see this listening device. It was his nature. I turned away and "Boom!" One of the officers tripped a trip wire and both died instantly. Dale was still alive. But barely. The Medic stayed with him, keeping him going until minutes into the dust off, he died. This was a very sobering moment to us all and we never conducted this type of mission again. This was the beginning, for me, of isolating myself from any new guys. This is what the FNG's called "The cold, distant, stare." The pain was too much. Dale was liked by everyone. The Dink's gave us a wide birth that day, and best they did, for revenge took precedence over anything else.

That night we loggered up in our NDP and held services for Dale. We were to guard a base vacated by some grunt outfit and to be turned over to the Arvin's the next day. We blew the hell out of everything, leaving little untouched. His best friend, Ray Rader, never knew the details until Kokomo, IN, in 1999 when we met for the first time in 29 years. To this day, some 30 plus years later, it's still very difficult to describe the moment as it is still very vivid and painful.

4/2/1970, Dale Andre Gronsky, Wakeman, OH, Explosive Device, 12W/81

4/8/1970, Paul Caven, Medic, The morning started out as many others did. As a medic in C-Troop 1/1 Cav, part of my job was to dispense salt tablets and malaria pills to the troops. Although many guys declined to take the pills, I was directed by SGT E-7 "Daddy Rabbit" Wilson to make sure the guys at least got them.

I didn't really know William Sharp but remember giving him the tablets. He seemed like a real nice guy who took his job very seriously.

We were out on a mission later that day, God knows where when Sharps APC was blown by a large command detonated mine. I believe he was driver for the motor track

I was on a track one or two tracks behind his. There was a large explosion with so much dust and smoke at first you could not see what happened. When the dust began to clear I could see the guys who were blown clear. There was one trooper who had a sever gash near his eye; otherwise everyone seemed to be very shaken but otherwise unhurt. I believe there may have been some ARVINS on the track also. Someone asked what happened to Sharp? Since he was the driver, he didn't get thrown clear and was pinned underneath the over turned APC. He was medavaced immediately as I could tell he was seriously injured. After he was medavaced, "Daddy Rabbit" asked me how I thought he would make out? I told him I did not think he would make it. He was upset at me for saying it. However, a few hours latter it was confirmed he had indeed expired.

I believe a memorial service along with an Easter Mass was given some days latter out in the field. It was the first American casualty I had witnessed. It wasn't to be my last unfortunately.

4/8/1970, William A Sharpe Jr, Tucson, AZ, Landmine, 12W/109

4/20/1970, Kenneth Allan Butler Jr, Kalamazoo, MI, Explosive Device, 11W/27

5/7/1970, Neal Lord, Whittier, CA, Landmine, 11W/126

Anthony John Newman, "Obsession,"
Midnight interlude with memories long past,
Turning and tossing, hoping it will soon pass.
Specters of comrades come to one's mind,
Having once loaded a cellophane coffin,
Regurgitated impressions come all too often.
Sweating profusely this nightly regime,
Guilt rides on night wings, will I ever be clean?
Push away loved ones with distasteful ease,
Does anyone hear my voice, please help me, please.

5/20/1970, Grant Coble, We were informed we would see action during a track commander meeting one evening in a place called Hiep Duc. This was a hot zone and we were going there. Little did we know just how much action at the time. This was about the time of the invasion of Cambodia. A Troop was going with us and we were to meet up with a company from the 196th once we were there.

Hiep Duc Valley is located west and maybe a little north of the city of Tam Ky. A small village stands at the mouth of the valley. We were also informed these people were armed militia and not to worry. This did not go down too well with us. There were 3 fire bases located on the south rim of the valley, LZ East, LZ Central, and LZ West. Our mission was search and destroy. The unit we would be facing was the 2nd NVA regiment.

We left Tam Ky fully loaded and headed out. Up the French Highway, turn onto a dirt road, and into the country side. Our normal plan of action was to trail the lead track, usually an ACAV (113). My tank was the second track in line. I was a prime target for any VC or NVA with an RPG. All was quiet on our way out. We did jump some VC in a small clearing, turned to engage, but were ordered to continue on. Why I will never

know? It may have been that the 196th was landing in a clearing at about 1:30 from our position and someone was afraid we might hit a friendly or a chopper taking off. This was known to happen and due care was needed.

Grant Coble setting in the TC hatch on a Sheridan Tank, Charlie 39.

We picked up the grunts near the entrance to the valley before the village. With 4 to 5 per track we continued on. We didn't see any villagers with weapons as we passed and this made us feel a little more at ease. A dirt road passed through the village and on into the valley. I was not real happy being in the position of lead as my main gun did not work. We had a canister round in the tube for what good that did. Several things had been tried to bring the main gun back on line but none worked.

Our first day and not a click into the valley when all hell broke loose. Coming into a draw, someone let us know they did not like us and sent a hail of rockets as greeting cards. We spun to the right and used machine guns on them. The ACAV in front did the same. The rest of the Platoon went up a knoll and watched the action, unable to respond as they couldn't see where the fire was coming from.

The grunts had already dismounted prior to the action and hit the ground when the action started. This little section I'm about to tell about involved one grunt with 9 lives. The infantry conduct battle differently than a Armored Cavalry unit does. We stand our ground and punch it out or charge the enemy. The grunts seek cover, return

Grant Coble

fire, and seek a way of resolving the issue with the enemy. One of the things a track does when taking RPG fire is race back and forth to confuse the enemy. The grunts didn't know this and one fellow laid in the paddy behind the tank. Guess he figured that might be a safe spot. As we backed up we ran him over once. We then went forward and ran him over again. What made matters worse, we stopped on top of him. At this moment one of his buddies jumped up, ran to the front of the tank and told the driver to pull ahead as we had just ran over the fellow. Pat Monahan did so and informed me of what had just happened. With everything else happening I must have not understood him (30 years later this story came to light) and continued on with the battle. What I do remember was ordering a grunt to tie the back pack onto the back so it would not fall off again. Little did I know at the time someone had been wearing that back pack.

The Grunt had laid down in one of the few soft spots in the paddy. When we ran him over we pushed him down into the mud. The second time we really planted him and only his back pack was visible. Several of his buddies pulled him out, covered with mud, and all he wanted was his rifle so he could shoot the tank crew. Richard Scales, a member of his squad, and on his first mission, filled us in on the details 30 some years later during a gathering in Kokomo, Indiana Vietnam Vets gathering. Later that day the grunt was dusted off. It was again 30 some years later another part of this story came to light when Dave Cooper told us this part. The grunt came into the aid station on Hawk Hill, all covered in mud; with mud packed into his nose and ears, still cussing and swearing at us. He stated he had been ran over by a tank, but no one would believe him.

One round hit just in front of the tank. Everything went black and to this day I do not remember the blast, only darkness, peace, and quiet. I've always wondered if this is what they mean by "Your life flashing before you?" As the air began to clear Pat came over the intercom screaming he was hit. Hell, I was too! I asked him how bad was it? Silence. I dropped to the seat below, dropped my pants and began to inspect my groin and thigh on my right leg. It hurt like hell, but hey, I had to make sure the family jewels were ok. Robbie Bowens and Vern Rexinger sat and stared in disbelief. I guess they figured they were dead men. I had a very large red welt across the inner part of my leg from a piece of shrapnel. I started to check the rest of me while the battle raged, oblivious to it. About this time Pat came back and said it was only mud that covered his face. He was lucky as the C-ration box next to him took a direct hit, disintegrating the spaghetti and meat balls and turning the pound cake to crumbs.

One of the most astonishing sights was a small Cessna Aircraft, 2 man, green wing over flying tree top high over the jungle in front of us. Here we are getting our asses shot off and this crazy Air Force guy, or Army, flies along at about 80 MPH, weaving back and forth, tipping his wing to see what is below. With the sun radiating down on us, and looking at the right spot, you could catch the gleam of a rocket streaking upwards towards the Cessna. He just kept on flying as if not a worry in the world. That wasn't the case for the NVA as the call came to "Duck!" Artillery shells erupted below his path. The pilot had called in Arty at the location of fire. That pilot had a pair of "Steel" balls.

He must have taken fire from the 1000 foot hill for with-in minutes the fast movers (jet bombers) came in with 1000 pounders and napalm and began pounding the side of the hill. It was rather humorous to hear that the pilots were whining that someone was shooting machine guns at them and wanted us to stop them! I always wondered what was wrong with that picture?

During our nightly defensive logger we took rocket fire. The rockets came from a hill overlooking our position, badly wounding one grunt. With the low cloud ceiling we could not get a chopper in and the grunt died of his wounds before dawn. This was only the beginning of a bad mission.

During the next day we tried moving to different locations and always under fire. Once the squad attached to us got pinned down and we backed up into the open, putting us between the enemy and the grunts and led them to safety using the tank as a shield.

5/20/1970, Paul Caven, Medic, May 20, 1970, was the worst day of my life to date. I may or may not have witnessed the death of David Vigil. I was with two troopers that day, the last day of their lives. I don't know their names or even it they were with C-Troop, but my account is as follows.

The day dawned upon us in the valley of Hiep Duc Valley. It was a scary place with downed helicopters, well made NVA bunkers, and I had a real bad feeling on this mission.

Shortly after dawn as we were to break from our night logger the RPG's, or rockets began to come down from the mountains. We were giving it back, but they seemed to "walk in" the RPG's and we had to scramble. There was much confusion, but things latter settled down. As we were stopped and there was a lull in the fighting, I was summoned that there was a Trooper down. It seems he was hit by one of our own high caliber weapons. He was almost cut in two be the round and there was no hope for him.

5/20/1970, David L Vigil, Granada, CO, Small Arms Fire, 10W/72

After that incident quieted down, I was summoned by the medic track that one of our troops was under intense fire and there was possible casualties.

I jumped into the back of the track and after a short ride we stopped. From there I walked in the back of the track until I saw some fallen troopers. As I was going to administer aid to one, I was knocked down by a round to the back and one to the forearm. I felt temporarily paralyzed but shortly the feeling began to return. I don't recall a lot of pain right away.

Another medic, a black guy who had just arrived in the troop days earlier came to my aid and was promptly killed with a head shot. As the combat was intensifying, I pulled the young medic over me and "played dead." Another medic, Alvin Whilow, also was dropped coming to our aid, though I don't think his wounds were mortal.

After the fighting quieted down and the feeling returned to my body, I continued to give aid to the many wounded resulting in me getting the Silver Star. I made sure I was the last one on the medavac chopper. We were just thrown on in a heap as the chopper lifted off firing its guns.

All I could think about was how young and brave the door gunners were. Being three days into my 21st birthday and being an E-4, I sometimes felt like the old man. Amazing!

I'm not sure who the black medic was, but he was surely brave. I've always wished I could have told his parents how he died and what a hero he was.

I hope he is up in heaven and smiling at us Old Troopers with all our aches, pains, and mental anguish.

The next week at the hospital was sheer hell fighting for my life and watching others do the same. I thanked god I was in one piece and was not burned. The painful screams were agonizing.

As a medic I had never seen an APC, much less rode on one. I wasn't familiar with the weapons, never saw a M-79 until someone gave me one, and wasn't up on the cavalry "lingo," yet I was treated with respect and have nothing but praise for the 1/1 Cavalry.

It was hard to write this, but if anyone will benefit by it, it will be well worth it.

Therefore, if sometimes I seem confused, it is probably because I was. The whole experience was so strange, it was as if it were a different lifetime.

5/20/1970, Grant Coble, That afternoon we began to work our way up to LZ East. The grunts were working the flanks when they came onto some bunkers. 3 were cut down. Our medic, Doc Gray ran to help them with no regard for himself and was cut down. An assault on the bunker, some grenades, and that was it. My tank along with several ACAV's pushed on to a large stand of trees to clear the area, then pulled back. We put Doc's body, lain on a stretcher, on the back of the tank and carried him to a dust off area. A flack jacket was over his head covering the head wound. That was a sad moment. He was not only a hero, but a fine person.

5/20/1970, Kenneth Mervin Gray, San Francisco, CA, Multiple Fragmentation Wounds, 10W/70

That evening we made the top of the hill and loggered for the night. All was quiet for the first time since we came into the valley, but the NVA, and we, knew we had to come down again, and we did.

Grant Coble

My last day in the fight started out with us out of water, a main gun that did not work, and a coax machine gun that did not work most of the time. In other words, we only had our personal weapons and the 50 cal to defend ourselves. Getting thirsty, I jumped off the side of the tank, hit the side of the dirt road, tumbled into the ditch, came up sore, and fell down again. Of all the things, I just broke my ankle. The medic must have seen this for when I looked to see if the column was moving here he came on the run, picked me up, placed me on the front of the tank, took off my boot, and was about to take off my sock when I grabbed him and told him to cut it off : it hurt like hell. I passed up on the dust-off's until evening. The next day I was wearing a cast on my right ankle which lasted 6 weeks.

A Troop suffered the most, between the armored units and the grunts, who came into the valley some 103 strong, left with 30 still able to function. Rick Scales survived as did the grunt we ran over. I lost a friend named Allen Parks, in A Troop, who I knew Stateside in college before the war. His track with 3 other Cavalry soldiers died when a RPG hit it and went up in flames.

5/27/1970, James Dean, Floyd started his tour in January of 1970, about the same time I did. He was a very tall African-American from Nashville, TN. I heard he played basketball in college, but they still drafted him. I do not remember what track he normally rode on, but do remember him applying for CO (conscientious objector) status. I also know that he stated that the VC/NVA had done nothing to him and he would not fight them. What do you do with an individual like this? He was still required to go to the field on missions. Did he pull his share of guard? Was he trusted? I don't know, because he did not ride on my track. I really can't say what he was like in the field. However I do know what happened this one day, 27 May, 1970.

On this day we were on mission in Heip Duc Valley. The Platoon had just cleared a tree-line and went on line. We were firing the hell out of this hillside that was right in front of us. My Track (C-32) was on the right flank. My driver (Allen Dixon) was maneuvering the track back and forth so as not to present a stationary target. My two M-60 gunners (can't remember their names) were firing away at the base of the hill as was I on the 50 Cal. One of my gunners started shouting something and I looked back. There was Floyd running toward my track and he's carrying his M-16. It seemed like he took only two more steps and he was in the cargo hatch area. I turned my attention back to the front and then decided to tell him (Floyd) to get down. Floyd was pretty tall plus he's now standing on two layers of ammo cans. I turned back, but before I could say anything I saw the bullet impact his steel pot just above the left ear. Blood started pouring out like a water hose and Floyd did a slow spiral to the floor. I keyed my helmet mike and requested a medic to C-32. The medic (can't remember his name) was on board in a flash. All this time Allen is still going back an forth in a zigzag pattern; my right gunner is assisting the medic, and I'm calling for a medivac while still firing the 50 cal. C-36 (Lt. Cuccia) tells me medivac is enroute and to fall back to the last clearing before the tree-line. I guided Allen in reverse until we could turn around and speed toward the clearing. The medic had Floyd's head encased in bandages and was giving him CPR. We got to the clearing an I think the medivac was just coming in along with another helicopter. We got Floyd loaded on the medivac an the medic went with him, all the time doing CPR. He was really trying to keep him going until he could get to the hospital. I knew he was hit real bad, but when I saw what was in the track floor, I knew he didn't have a chance.

I'm getting ready to rejoin the platoon when the squadron CO (LTC Graves) came and informed me I was to remain in place. He had re-supply helicopters inbound and needed me to call them in. I can't remember how many drops they did, but there was ammo, fuel, an water billets all over the place. This is where I stayed until the Troop came back from the mission. Floyd died at the hospital. The medic did his very best, but with the loss of blood and everything else it wasn't meant to be. I guess sometimes you don't realize when your being shot at. When Allen started looking at the track all the drivers periscopes were shot and the trim vane was full of bullet holes.

5/27/1970, Charles D Floyd, Nashville, TN, Small Arms Fire, 10W/108

Anthony John Newman, "Burden,"

Snaking and skulking, with inordinate care,
Quietly with stealth, nobody knows you are there.
Your target appears not the least bit suspect,
He pauses a moment and lights a cigarette.
A fine-tooled weapon of death you possess,
One shot - one kill, death without excess,
Fine hairs are crossed marking with care,
One whose life will soon not be there.
Softly and gently, not a jerk - not a bump,
Squeeze very carefully an hear the "crack-thump."
Confirmation they need to know how we fare,
He's dead, just a child, does nobody care?
Live with this my civilian friends,
Live with this burden of one who defends.

5/30/1970, Randall "Hillbilly" Densmore, We had just came back from fighting in Hiep Duc. One of the tanks that had been in the field with us had not fired a round and was being worked on when we got back. I was the driver for Lt. Cuccia; this is one day I will never forget. We had just loggered down when Cuccia said to me, "Hillbilly, clean out the track while I go shave and get cleaned up." He started walking away, and the gun on the tank that was being worked on fired and hit Lt. Cuccia. He died on the spot. I helped put him in the body bag, then picked up his arm an placed it in the bag with him.

5/30/1970, Dominick Cuccia, Huntington Station, NY, Accident, 10W/120

1970, LTC Cosbie Saint, Squadron Commander

6/10/1970, Grant Coble, I was still wearing the solid cast when the Platoon Mess was relocated to Hill 29. We were to manage as best we could by going to either A Troop or HQ for chow. As HQ was a very long walk, I elected to go to A Troop's mess to eat. This was the only time. I stood in line waiting my turn and as I slowly approached the door, the flies got thicker. Inside, it was bad. I was very hungry; otherwise I'd have left. I took the chance and ate the food which wasn't too good, but filling. Next day I began my toughest battle. Got up and was about to head to the shower when another pressing issue led me to the outhouse. It was a busy place that morning as we all had ate in A Troop. I sat and quickly relieved myself, but with some discomfort as cramps took over. I had the shits, or better know as the "GI's." The outhouses became "over crowded" during the next few days until we got some meds to cure the problem. It was not unusual for the 4 hollers to be filled and several guys could be seen squatting in the sand near by. But, 2 bottles of Petal-Bismal later, supplied by Tim Bunge, and I was back to myself. A Troops Mess hall was shut down for health reasons.

6/17/1970, Charles Deo Maloney, Altoona, PA, Explosive Device, 9W/60

6/1970, Carl Wronko, Enjoyed the leave. I said a real good-bye to the family and went to Newark Airport to fly to San Francisco. In SF, stayed one night in a hotel room, went to the Air Force Base in Oakland and got on the plane. Arrived in Vietnam, at Ton Sa Nut Air Base after stopping in Alaska and Japan. Really, didn't feel like a tourist. We were greeted by a military reception: or, rather, a group of guys who had just finished their tour. They were on the way home, and had some not very nice things to say to cheer us up. It didn't work, we weren't cheerful.

Went to the replacement area fully expecting to be assigned to the Infantry or the 11th Armored Cav. Really wanted the 11th as it was a famed outfit with a fine reputation for its work in Vietnam. May as well be with the best, I thought. However, given the Jungle School training, I figured its going to be an Infantry Assignment. We are told to look at the BOARD each morning, noon and afternoon for an assignment. The scuttlebutt is, whatever happens, pray that you don't get assigned up North where the hardcore NVA carry most of the battle. The very next day, I look at the BOARD and see my name. I follow the line across my name to see that I am assigned to something called the Americal Division. OK. Where and what is that? I'd heard of all the Army Divisions in Vietnam and didn't recall that one. I go up to the Sgt. in charge of my group and inquire. Why that Division is up NORTH and its Lt. Callys old Division. Great, it's up north and it's the army Division with the worst reputation. So, I gather my newly issued belongings and head to the Airport for the flight up.

I arrive in a place called Chu Lai Air Base which is right on the South China Sea. Pass under a sign that says welcome to the Americal Division and board a duce and a half truck to be driven to another replacement area. Another sign, welcoming me to the Americal. Well, at least they are friendly. I sign in, am assigned to a hooch (what's a hooch and where do I go to get it?), find out that it is a shed like structure surrounded by barrels, that I'm supposed to sleep in.

They start giving us some instruction on how to stay alive in the Americal AO. Every one, but the future clerks and the jerks, pays strict attention to this stuff. We're not on the way to Vietnam, we are HERE! We train for several days. We see VC, who had turned themselves in, crawl through barbed wire without making a sound or shaking a can. Everyone cheers his skill. I don't. This guy is good but then so are his buddies who did not surrender. We are told in a class for Officers only about something called fragging, where someone in your own unit tries to kill you by using a hand grenade, a rifle, or a clamor, if they don't like you. The instructor, who is an officer, tells a story about the death of a Platoon Leader who had just recently been killed when he walked in front of a tank and the main gun went off, supposedly accidentally. Moral of the story, do a good job but watch your ass. We are also told to look to the BOARD again for our assignments.

Is it going to be Armor or Infantry? Neither, it's a Cavalry outfit called the 1st Squadron 1st Armored Cavalry Regiment of Dragoons. I'm thrilled. I'm not going to be a grunt after all. I'm going to make it home alive. Thank you Lord. I go see the Sgt. In charge: they have one of these all over the place in Vietnam, and tell him of my assignment and inquire as to how I get there. He tells me he'll call the unit and they will come for me. He also tells me this is the unit where the Platoon Leader had been killed by the main gun going off. A bit of a downer, that piece of information. After a while a jeep shows up for me and off I go to the home base of the 1/1 Armored Cav.

When I get there they put me in a temporary hooch, I go to meet the Squadron Commander, a Lt. Col. Graves, and I am told he is the finest. The Col. asks what I am doing at the present time. I tell him

I'm waiting to hear which Troop I will be assigned to. He says to follow him. He gets on a helicopter and I jump on after him. It's the Col., his S-3 Captain, and me. Off we go. They are wearing helmets and can speak to each other, but I have no idea what is going on, as I sit there holding on for dear life.

After a good while, the Col. points down and we go down like an elevator. I look out the door and see what looks like a big rock pile; I mean a real big rock pile. At the base of the rock pile, I see armored vehicles and men walking around them. The door gunner opens up on the rocks. The chopper drops lower almost to the ground. The Col. points at me and then the seat. I'm supposed to stay there. OK, wasn't going to get out anyway. He and the Captain jump out onto the top of this hill. The chopper takes off. I see them shooting at something. Damned if I can see what it is. I later learned it took time to adapt your eyes to look sharp to see what was around you. Down goes the chopper, the Col. and Captain throw two bleeding, but non-moving bodies of Viet Cong on, and then jump on themselves. They are carrying their own M-16s and two AK-47s. My eyes are seeing things now.

The chopper stays in the area for a while longer as the men from the armored vehicles are working their way up that pile of rocks. Then we leave the area. Go someplace and they dump off the bodies; I'm still sitting in that seat until I'm told otherwise. We go back to the Cav area; the Col., the Captain, and an extremely pale faced 2nd Lt. jump off. The Col. tells me I'll do fine and welcome to his unit He'll see me around and to go to the S-1 shop for my assignment. If that's what he wants done, that's what I am going to do.

They tell me in the personnel section that I am assigned to C Troop; and, that a jeep will be by for me shortly. I get my stuff; the jeep finds me and takes me to the C Troop rear area in Chu Lai. Here I meet Scott Lafavor, the Troop XO, short for Executive Officer, and he takes me to the Platoon Leader's hooch, helps me store my state side military and civilian clothing and turns me over to the Supply Sgt. to draw more equipment. I am to join him in the Orderly Room when I get done, which I do. I meet the First Sgt. The XO tells me I will be the Platoon Leader for the Third Platoon as the 1st and 2nd Platoons already have Lts. No problem. I ask about the LT who had been the 3rd Platoon Leader, did he DEROS or was he given a rear area job? I'm told, "No, he had died when he walked in front of the main gun of a Sheridan Tank which was being worked on, and it fired accidentally when the mechanic had done something wrong." Immediate flashback to the fragging class. Maybe, if I ask nicely, I can still get that Infantry assignment. The XO and I go back to his hooch. The Troop is due in the next day for a stand down or a week off to do major maintenance on the vehicles, so I will not chopper out to the Troop, but will meet my Platoon then.

    I spent a nice night thinking everything over, the chain of events that had brought me here, the dead Platoon Leader whose Platoon I would very soon be in charge of, and how I would approach them in the morning. I did verify later that Lt. Dominick L Cuccia (Wall Panel 10W, Line 120) had died as I was told and had not been killed by the men of 3rd Platoon. I also thought of some advice my uncle had given me before I left home. Uncle Joe had been an Infantry Sgt. during WW2, landed on D-Day with the Big Red One and made it through the entire campaign - he and only one other guy from the original company. He had told me that the Army had done the best they could to train me, but despite all that I didn't know shit. He advised me to latch on to a senior Sgt. who knew his stuff, who had been in country for a while, to listen, watch and learn; and if everything went well, I just might make it home alive and the men who would be in my Platoon just might make it home alive as well. He also advised to listen to the men in the Platoon as they had been there, and just might know something that would benefit me and educate me. Sounded like good advise when he had given it to me, and I decided, lying in that empty hooch in Chu Lai, Vietnam that it was still sound advise and I would begin to act on it in the morning. What I didn't appreciate at the time was that my uncle was absolutely correct. Despite my training, the Army had never before actually placed me in a leadership position. Since my commissioning all I had done was go through Army Schools and then I had been a Training Officer and a fancy tour guide. I had never led a Platoon in any capacity, which was the primary purpose of a Lieutenant in the Army, never mind in combat capacity, and I was going to have

Dragoons

to learn fast, I.e. good ole Army on the job training. But, they say, ignorance is bliss, and I was as blissful as could be.

The Platoon that would shortly become my responsibility was an armored Cavalry Platoon. A cavalry Platoon had changed in make up over the course of the war in Vietnam. Originally, the platoon was equipped, at least on paper, with three heavy M-48 Battle Tanks and seven Armored Cavalry vehicles which were modified M-113 personnel Carriers and referred to as ACAVs. An Infantry Squad was carried within one of the PCs. By mid 1970, the time of my arrival in Vietnam, the M-48 tanks had been replaced by M-155 Sheridan Light Amphibious Tanks and the Infantry Squad element was no more. In theory the Platoon still consisted of three Sheridan Tanks and seven ACAVs, one of which was equipped with a mortar, thus "The Motor Track."

The ACAV had become a pure fighting platform. It's crew consisted of a driver, a Track Commander (TC) who rode on the vehicles cupola, two side gunners, one on each side riding a jeep seat (which were not Army issue but scrounged), and depending upon manpower another soldier riding on the rear hatch armed with a Grenade Launcher (affectionately called a Blooper) or an M-16 Rifle. The firepower was provided by a 50 Caliber Machine Gun operated by the TC, behind the forward gun shield; two M-60 Machine Guns, each with a gun shield, operated by two gunners, and the rifle or blooper of the extra soldier, if the track had one. Each crew member also had their own M-16 Rifle. When dismounted troops were needed for a search mission or a patrol, one or both of the gunners as well as the other soldier would be available. Well it was, if you considered about 2 inches or so of reinforced aluminum as Armor. It would stop an AK-47 round and mortar or grenade shrapnel. But I wouldn't want to hide in it with someone firing a 50 Cal. Machine gun at it, never mind an RPG; nor, be inside of it when it ran over a mine.

The Sheridan Tank was crewed by a driver, a Tank Commander riding in the vehicles cupola and firing a machine gun, behind a forward gun shield, a gunner and loader (depending upon manpower there may only have been one of these), both of whom rode on the top of the Tank rather than inside due to the effects of a mine blast. The crew each carried an M-16 rifle as well. The armor that protected it was a combination of aluminum and a Styrofoam like substance, for the most part, on the side. The idea was, I think, to have the RPG explode against the metal and then have the Styrofoam absorb the blast. Actually, this worked better than the 'hard' armor of the old tanks and it was safer in that regard. The main gun, a 155MM, was the most devastating weapon carried by the platoon. Rounds fired from it in Vietnam were of 3 varieties; a Can Round or Flashette Round made up of thousands of tiny nail like metal pieces which blasted from the main gun like a shotgun; a High Explosive Round or HE, and a Heat Round, or Black Death.

The terrain reach of the platoon was remarkable. The tracks could function in a jungle environment, open plains, sandy beaches, rice paddies, and hilly environments. Just about everywhere a foot soldier could go, so could an armored cavalry platoon, but with much greater firepower.

Third Platoon, C Troop, First Squadron, First Cavalry Regiment of Dragoons, (The Blackhawk Regiment) enters my life.

The next morning I awoke and joined the XO for breakfast at the C Troop Mess Hall and have absolutely no recollection of what I had to eat. I next recall standing with the XO by the Troop Headquarters and watching the Troop pull in to the Troop AO. There were about 24 to 30 Armored Vehicles pulling in and then lining up in one long contiguous line, facing the same direction. As we stood there, the Troop Commanding Officer came over, I think I saluted, and we went into the Quonset hut containing his office. Thus I met John LaRoche, Captain in the Armor Branch, graduate of West Point and on his second tour of Vietnam. He had been Troop Commander for two months by this time and was confident of his abilities. We would become a fine team in time. If I recall correctly, he asked me about my experience state side, how I was commissioned, and then called for the Platoon Sergeant of 3rd Platoon.

In walked Sgt. First Class Ruben Thomas. We were introduced. Thomas had only been with the Platoon for a short while, having arrived in Vietnam after a tour in an Armor Unit in Germany. He had been the Platoon Leader since the death of my predecessor in May. We took our leave of the CO and walked outside together and began to talk. He wanted to fill me in about the Platoon. What he had to say did cause me some concern from the beginning. The men had not reacted well to him, did not respond to his direction, considered him "To stateside" in his methods, and he had had his hands full. Thomas and I would develop a very effective working relationship as time went on. I handled the operation and tactics of the platoon and he took care of logistics and maintenance. By the time he left me, he told me that the Army was his career, that he had been in over ten years, and considered me the second best platoon leader that he had ever served with during those years. I always regretted, in later years, not asking him why I was only number two in his experience. I have always respected him and appreciated all he did for the 3rd Platoon and me.

"Well Sergeant," I said, "Thanks for the heads up. Its time to go meet the Platoon, lets do it," and we walked out and over to the parked tracks of 3rd Platoon. Sgt. Thomas called the men over. I didn't know it, but I was about to add to the shocks that I had been receiving since arriving in Vietnam.

From around, atop and inside of the vehicles, a mass of men started moving toward us, about 30 or so if my memory serves me right. What greeted me was not exactly what I had been expecting. All were very young, bare headed, most not wearing a shirt, some had on rolled up fatigue pants, some were in sandals rather than boots, and around most of their necks were what I later learned to be peace symbols and love beads. One young Trooper had a ferret hanging in his neck - nice pet as they kill rats. For a moment I thought I had been transported from Vietnam to Woodstock, but I would learn in time that first impressions were not accurate. No one said anything, they just looked. Time for me to say something, but what do I say to this group. Considering what Thomas had told me about his troubles with them, I decided only one way to do it, and that was to say it straight. It's been over 30 years so I can't quote myself verbatim. I was keenly aware that they all knew that the people back in the US, for the most part did not support the war, that the President of the US had already declared the withdrawal of American Forces, and that no one wanted to die in support of a lost cause. They simply wanted to get home in one piece. So I told them that I needed their help to get us all home alive, that I would do my very best to accomplish that. I admitted that they knew more than I did about how an Armored Cavalry Platoon should operate in Vietnam, that I would use what I had learned in training but I would be open to their ideas and suggestions. We would try to accomplish the missions assigned to us but in a manner not likely to cause casualties amongst us. I let them know that I expected the very best out of them as well, that we had to work as a team to make our Platoon sharp and combat efficient; and, that we had to look out for each other both in combat and in the day to day running and maintaining of the Platoon, so we would together be ready for combat when it came.

When I finished, there was no applause, no pats on the back, no 'we are behind you LT.' These were combat veterans, and I was still a green 2nd Lt. Words would not suffice, they wanted to see deeds. And, so it began. They returned to their tracks and I had the Senior Sergeants stay behind, and we talked about what would be accomplished during that stand-down, both from a maintenance and training viewpoint, I repeated my invitation for ideas and suggestions. At that time, I quickly began to appreciate the knowledge and flair of Staff Sgt. Earl Verigan who commanded the lead Track. During the stand-down I watched and listened and learned. I think they appreciated my questions and interest. I began to get input. My crew took to me. The Platoon Leader's ACAV was number C-36 and his, now my, call sign would be Charlie 36.

Anthony John Newman, "F.N.G.,"
"Newbee," "Fanough," "F.N.G.,"
What are all these people saying about me?
In their faded green jungles
All disheveled, what a sight,
I haven't learned the rules of war,
I haven't learned to fight.
They stare at me distrustingly,
They don't know me from the rest.
I haven't stood the ring of fire.
I haven't passed their test.

Steve George was the C-36 Track Commander or TC; Randall 'Hillbilly' Densmore was the C-36 Driver, and Norman 'Red' Bourgault was the side gunner. Steve would be with me for about one mission and then he would be transferred to the Troop Commander's Track and replaced by Mike Sargo who would finish his tour with me. Randall would also be with me for the balance of his tour both in the field and then as my jeep driver when I was later transferred to the XO position. Needless to say we got to be good friends, when I could understand him and his strong "Hillbilly" accent. He'd always let me know what he thought, whether I wanted to hear it or not. Red would be with me about half way through my tour as Platoon Leader, he was from Maine and his accent was about as bad as Hillbillies. Frankly, I don't know how they ever communicated even speaking the same language.

Anyway, the crew of my track began to train me. First they let me know that I was expected to handle the M-60 machine gun on my side of the track. They showed me how the ammo was stored and how to get at it. They got me a water tight ammo box to put my personal belongings in, showed me how to use the intercom system for the Platoon and the Troop, where to keep my M-16 rifle, told me not to wear underwear to avoid crotch rot, and let me know in many subtle ways that I was expected to pull my own weight. They strapped down the second antenna on the track. All the ACAVs and Sheridans in the platoon had one antenna. The Platoon Leader's track had two, one for communication with the Platoon and a second for communication with the Troop Commander. Two antennas in the air would be a dead give away to the enemy - this is the Platoon Leader's Track - so they strapped one down. I first thought, "Hey, they must be beginning to like me, they are trying to protect me." Later, it dawned on me that they were also riding on that ACAV and that they had no interest in being a special target either. But, it felt good at the moment.

My education about how to act in the field also began. "Don't go down the middle of a bowling alley, or over the top of a hill," was one of the first. That translated into, never take your Platoon right down the middle of a valley between two hills or over the tops of hills - always drive around the sides of the hills. Why? Mines are placed in the obvious lanes of travel. In the valleys and on the tops of hills where the view is good. Mines can be more readily seen on the sides of hills where the rain can wash away the dirt. Next came, always track the vehicle in front of you. That meant each succeeding track would drive in the track marks left by the track in front of you, which was a great way to avoid mines. You could feel fairly safe if the lead track did not blow up by staying in its track marks. Now I wasn't a driver but they wanted me to know this so when we got new guys in I'd be sure they followed this rule. My next lesson was similar to this. When we stopped for the night we'd form a logger or a circle with the guns pointed out. If you got down off the track, in an unsecured area, it was a good idea to walk in the track marks so you'd miss any mines that might still be there. I'll mention more lessons and advice as I go along.

I wish I could give the names of the individuals who advanced my education but after thirty plus years I can't. I can say that it was a group effort. They also began to teach me a new language. One that was particular to Troops in Vietnam and that had been honed even more for use by Troops in combat or field units that actually engaged the enemy in battle. Some of the words used and there meaning is given throughout. A further small sampling of the words and phrases: dee dee (get going or move); dee dee mau (get going or move faster); the World (home, America, any place but Vietnam); wasted (killed); "don mean nothing" (down play of a bad event); chop chop (food - usually C rations); mamma san (woman); papa san (man); baby san (baby or young child); boom-boom (sex - usually paid for); dink (Vietnamese or VC - used interchangeably); ville (village or group of huts); short timer (soldier with only a few days left in Vietnam - usually begun at the half-way mark); "there it is" (used in agreement with a statement); lifer (career NCO or Officer); bac I (medic, nurse or Doctor); ti ti (little or small); six (Troop or Company Commander - usually a Captain); shake and bake (a graduate of the NCO school, instant Sergeant); and, butter bar (Second LT.)

7/7/1970, Raymond Raliford Mays, Okeechobee, FL, Rocket, 3W/103

8/1970, After the stand down was over in about a week, the Troop left to return to the field. To elaborate on a 'stand down', the squadron was made up of three troops. The troops were usually, barring a major operation, rotated in the field so that at any one time there were two in the field and one back in the rear. The troop in the rear would pull maintenance on the armored vehicles and provide further rear security if the stand down was being held at the Squadron's forward base at Hawk Hill, rather than at the division ear area in Chu Lai where there were no security obligations. It also provided an opportunity for the field troopers to get some much needed rest and relaxation. In Chu Lai there were Quonset huts with real cots in them; at Hawk Hill there were bunkers with cots in them. At Chu Lai, the troops were also taken to a beach on the South China Sea run by the USO for more relaxation. We also would have a cookout and beer blast for them during this time. It was interesting how the troopers paired off in the rear. Usually by races, blacks with blacks and whites with whites; and, also, the beer drinkers (juicers) in one hut and the drug users (heads) in another. They would visit amongst each other but 'lived' with their own kind so to speak.

I remember walking into a hut occupied by 'heads' one time and seeing them smoking their pipes and joints. They didn't know I was coming and I had yet to learn of the drug use. I took a look, realized what was going on and just turned around and left without saying anything. I did not report what I saw or press the issue. It's not that I condoned drug use or excess drinking, but these young men were under tremendous stress. Forgotten by their countrymen, unappreciated by the South Vietnamese; fighting a war that we were in the process of losing as a result of their country abandoning its commitment, being in the field when 9 out or 10 other US soldiers in Vietnam had much safer rear jobs, and with no one to turn to except their own, they needed space and I gave it to them. I never saw any use of drugs or alcohol in the field and that is where it mattered. I later was called as a character witness for one of my troopers who had been caught with drugs after he had been assigned to a rear post. I told the court martial panel that he had been a fine trooper and that I would take him back in a minute to the field with me. With the expectation that he would not use drugs in the field. If he did, I would not have had to take action. His fellow troopers would have handled it as his conduct, while in the field, affected the well being of not just him but of his entire track crew and platoon members.

When the Troop left for the field after I joined, it road marched from Chu Lai, which was the Americal Division's home base, up Route 1, the only paved road in the country, through the City of Tam Ky. It either went out to Hawk Hill, which was the home base of the 1/1 Armored Cav, or else it made a left turn somewhere north of Tam Ky and headed out into the lowlands that the Troop patrolled. I don't remember which route was taken on my first field trip. Basically, our area of operations was between the mountains and the South China Sea. As we left the Troop area in Chu Lai, the Troop Commander had one of the other platoons lead off. He then followed with the next platoon after him and then my platoon bringing up the rear. I later found out from my Troopers that this was the preferred position because when you were last in line you were least likely to make contact or hit a mine. So following the route noted above, we went out to the field. I am not sure but I think we remained tail end Charlie for the next several days.

I got to experience a night logger and pulling a watch myself. We set up the RPG screen, which was a piece of chain link fencing, in front of the ACAV. It was designed to cause a Rocket Propelled Grenade to detonate early before hitting the ACAV or one of us. If it was raining a tarp was put up to the rear of the track by that lowered rear door to keep out of the rain. Cots to sleep on were set up, which impressed me as I expected to have to sleep on the ground. I was reinforcing my belief that it was much better to be in Armor than the Infantry. My crew again made sure I pulled my weight. We assigned the guard watches for the night and I received mine. Steve George asked me to contribute a C-Ration one night. He then proceeded to take one from each of the crew members and proceeded to make a 'stew' by combining them all into one pot, throwing in tobasco sauce, cheese and God knows what else. I admit that it was very tasty and filling.

After several days, Captain LaRoche told me to have my platoon take over as the lead. It was here that Sgt. Earl Verigan began to further my training. One thing I had learned in Infantry OCS was how to read a map. I'd been following the Troops course on the map I'd been given for several days, and felt I was reasonable able to read it and tell where we were located. Earl, who was the lead track

TC, told me to not direct him as to every change in course. Rather, he told me to pick out a terrain feature in the distance, which was in the direction I wanted to go, and then he would head toward it, picking the route as he went. In this way, I had an experienced NCO choosing the actual route. When we got to a point where it was necessary to change direction, I would speak to him on the radio and tell him left or right and give him the new terrain feature to head to. The system worked well and I used it the entire time I was the Third Platoon Leader even when we changed TCs. After Earl Verigan was transferred from the Platoon, I had Jim Dean take over the lead track position, and he and I also worked this system well together. I should mention the lead track TC was always the one who was felt to be the best, as our lives depended, on many occasion, on the course he choose. Both Verigan and Dean were, to use an old Army phrase, outstanding at it.

8/1970, Grant Coble, My last mission was to the Pineapple Forest. We had a new Platoon Sergeant named Thomas. He was a green as they get and came from a re-supply unit. This worried me greatly. What made matters worse was Lt. Wronko wanted me, a short timer, to train him. This meant I was to become a driver and that made me real unhappy. The SGT had a lot of questions and I, a lot of answers. When moving I would update him on what to look for and what to do should something happen. When stopped, the same. He was one nervous dude. I guess it must have paid off for many years later during one of our gatherings the LT. said Thomas did very well.

I remember someone telling a story about guys getting short and in the field. They became dangerous not only to others, but themselves. Reason being, over cautious, and I was getting that way. I tried to guard against this but not too well.

I was sent back to base camp on Hill 29 during the mission which was fine with me. My orders were to take charge of those from 3rd Platoon while there. This was no big deal as there were only a handful of us. One afternoon one of the Platoon Sgt's. ordered us to work on their tracks and get them ready for the field. All this time and not ready? Hummmm!? We worked up until almost dark when ordered to stand down. Now, I'm wasn't real happy being ordered to work on their tracks and as Acting Jack, took a stand. Me, "No, I don't think so." Him, "What do you mean?" Me, "We worked on your tracks and now you'll work on ours." I don't think this went down too well as he and the Motor Sergeant got into my face real bad. Them, "Article 15." Me, silently, "Oh Shit!" Now here comes the XO who once filled in, "Article 15 hell, court martial." Levenworth, here I come. My friend, Tim Bunge, over heard all this and, as he worked in TOC, contacted the Captain in the field. I returned to my cot, sat down, and pondered my future. Wasn't 15 minutes and here comes Tim. "Grant, your going to the rear. The Captain doesn't know what the job will be, but you are to take orders from only him or Top. Get your stuff together as you are leaving in the morning.' "My God, I'm out of the field!" This is every combat soldiers dream and not what I'd expected. Some one "Pinch" me!

For the next 5 of 6 weeks I had left in Vietnam was working in the Arms room repairing weapons and logging in new FNG's. I wasn't too sympathetic towards them. Years later I really wished I'd been more thoughtful. It was really neat to meet these guys some 30+ years later at our first reunion.

One night a bunch of us decided to steal Tops ¾ ton truck and go party. We hit what ever clubs we could find and drank to our hearts content. Our party atmosphere must have rubbed off as others joined in and by the wee hours of the morning, HQs was a shambles. I can only remember a few events of that night. We went from hooch to hooch drinking what ever was to be found. Who ever was present thus joined in and on to the next. Blind drunk and barely able to walk, we found the truck and somehow navigated back home. Guess we must have been a little noisy as Top came storming out of his hooch and yelled, "What the Hell!" We scattered. I missed breakfast that morning.

A new First Shirt came to our unit that day. He was given my extra bed to hang his hat until Scott left. 2 nights later Scott broke in the new guy right. In the wee hours of the morning here they came, blind drunk and raising hell. "Open the dam door, Grant!", came Scotts yell. I was still recovering from our party and wasn't ready to enjoy a drink yet. The two of them sat there joking, laughing, telling stories, and finishing off some beer I had in a small refrigerator. "I know you were one of the ones who stole my truck the last night so enjoy the moment as I did." "I did."

8/1970, Carl Wronko, Well when we took over as lead platoon, the CO told me to go to a particular spot on the map to search a village or ville. Off we went, and when I got to what I thought was the right place, I stopped and the Platoon went on line around the ville. LaRoche called me up and asked if I thought I was at the right place. I told him that I not only thought it but that we were at the right place. In fact we were at the right place!. We proceeded to search the ville. My reward was that 3rd Platoon was kept as the lead platoon for the balance of the entire mission instead of rotating platoons as was normal. I didn't realize it at first but this wasn't going over well with my Troopers. Being the lead platoon wasn't so much an honor as it was an invitation to be the first to hit a mine or make contact with the enemy. It was more stressful to be out front instead of bring up the rear. Since I had invited input from my platoon, one or more of them, I don't recall who, let me know that the practice in the past was to rotate the lead platoon and then suggested that I should remind the CO about this. Not an easy thing to do. I was a 2nd Lt. on my first mission with my new platoon and new CO; it wasn't likely that the CO would care to have my input on his operation of his Troop.

How to handle it? Easy, as we used to say, what's he going to do, 'send me to Vietnam?' Next time we stopped to logger for the night I made my way over to the CO's track and took a seat. He asked what I wanted, so I said, "I'm told the practice in the past was to rotate each platoon in and out of the lead platoon position, and your not doing that anymore and I think you should to give 3rd Platoon a break." I think the response was short and brief, something along the lines of, "Get lost and if I want any input from you I'll ask for it." "But...", I started, and got an immediate reply of, "Leave now young 2nd Lieutenant."

We not only were kept in the lead Platoon position, but he began to give us separate platoon size missions away from him, and on our own, where we were also obviously the Lead Platoon. He kept the other two platoons with him. I knew that this would not be the end of this developing circumstance. Then to add frosting to the cake, or perhaps I should say dust to the 3rd, when we began to return for a stand-down after either my very 1st or 2nd mission with the Troop, he called me up on the radio. "Are you still tired of being the lead platoon?", came the question. "Yes," was my response. "OK, pull to the side and pick up the tail end." With that, he began the return to our home base. This entailed traveling cross-country and picking up the "Red Ball" which was a purely dirt road, red in color from the dirt and dust all over that part of Vietnam. We began to travel the "Red Ball." It was the dry season and in no time at all we were eating the red dust thrown up from the tracks of the 1st, 2nd, and HQ. Platoons. I mean it was all over the ACAVs, the Sheridans, our equipment, and us. Really wasn't a nice thing to do to his best platoon. My boys were not 'happy' and I was not happy either. I could just feel the tension building. The Troop next came to the Black Ball, or paved Highway 1 and turned onto it heading toward Tam Ky and then on to Chu Lia.

What was going to happen? It didn't take long to find out as we approached the town of Tam Ky. I noticed my Track TC looking back over his shoulder. When I turned to see what he was looking at, I saw that some smoke grenades had been tossed over onto the side of the road from the ACAVs and Sheridans bringing up the rear. All pretty yellows, greens, and reds. People were running from their homes and shops, which were right along side the highway, crying and shaking their fists at us. Mixed in amongst the colored smoke were CS Grenades, or for those not familiar, tear gas. All hell was now breaking lose, grenades were 'falling' off all of the Tracks from front to rear in our Platoon's column. I'm not sure, but I picked up a smoke or CS grenade to waive it at my guys to demonstrate that they should not be doing this, but it slipped from my hand as well. There we were, red dust all over everything, hauling ass through Tam Ky and watching the little people, tears streaming down their faces, dancing all over the place, amongst the now merging clouds of colored smoke and tear gas. Sherman may have marched through Georgia but 3rd Platoon Charlie Troop was now doing a job on the city of Tam Ky. When we cleared Tam Ky everything calmed down until we got to the entrance gate to the Americal Division Base Camp at Chu Lia. As we approached it, I saw the Troop Commander's

ACAV and some MP's standing there by the gate. Apparently, someone had radioed ahead about the events in Tam Ky. Well he was not happy, and I imagine his superiors were not too pleased either. But there I was covered in red dust with streaks of red down my face from the tears I had shed, or from laughing, I forget. Had to come up with something real fast. No problem.

I told him, as he went ballistic, that it was an obvious case of self-defense. VC infiltrators had throw grenades at us as we passed through the town. Not wanting to return fire, or throw hand grenades back, in a crowded town, my Troopers had done the next best thing in order to drive the VC away from the Highway and our vehicles without endangering the town's people. I was proud of them and their quick response and ingenuity. We were heroes. We had saved lives and property. We should be rewarded. Instead, we were kicked out of the Troop. The next day, I was told in private that the CO wasn't buying my bullshit. He threw my platoon out of C Troop. We were made to paint over our blue squares on our ACAVs, and blue markings on our Sheridan Tanks, with black paint. We were the 'Outcasts.' We absolutely loved it. For at least the next mission to the field we operated separately from Charlie Troop; and we did so with black squares and marking on our tracks. The CO did give us our missions and objectives but we were on our own. We moved by ourselves and we loggered at night alone. We relied only on each other. Moral was never higher. Pride in our platoon was rampant. When I think of all the events that happened during the first part of my tenor as 3rd Platoon Leader, this was the defining moment that brought us together and made us the tightly knit Platoon that we became. It also solidified my position as their LT. I had defended them. I had stood by them, and I was now one of them. Hell, if I had admitted what had happened, I'd have been relieved.

I should explain that the Squadron was made up of 3 separate Troops. In order to identify the separate Troops physically a color system was used. The tracks and tanks in each troop were painted with a different color marking. Red was for A Troop, white for B Troop, and C Troop had blue colored squares painted on the rear sides of the ACAVs and blue circles on the gun barrels of the Sheridans. Well, we no longer were in the color scheme of things.

Grant Coble

We had black squares and circles on our vehicles. We belonged only to ourselves. We were different. We had thumbed our noses at the green machine.

8/1970, Staff. Sergeant (E-6) Earl Verigan was a superb soldier. I have mentioned him before in this narrative. He was the TC of my lead track and taught me many things, which made me a better Platoon Leader than I believe I otherwise would have become. We worked very well together. 3rd Platoon was patrolling an area by ourselves. I received a radio message that the VC had ambushed an American Infantry unit in an area not far from where we were. The terrain must have been such so as to mask the sounds of that fight, as I could hear nothing. I let Verigan know what was happening an that we were going to head there to see if we could add our firepower to help the American unit. I gave him the direction to head an off we went. I believe the same terrain features that masked the sounds of the fighting also masked the sounds of the approach of our armored vehicles.

As we came up to the area where the fighting was, we could see the positions of each of the participants. The enemy saw us and broke to their rear in the only direction opened to them, which took them up a grassy hill right in front of us. There was a tree line at the top of that hill which they were heading toward for concealment and protection. Between my Tracks and the enemy was a gully with a stream in it so that we could not advance directly at them. I told Verigan to continue on with his ACAV and the Sheridan behind him to the right where he could cross the stream and come up from behind toward the enemy. This maneuver would also place these vehicles between the fleeing enemy and the ambushed American unit. I quickly brought the rest of our Sheridans and ACAVs on line facing toward the hill the enemy was moving up an opened fire on them. This stopped some of them who took cover, killed some of them, and made others move quicker toward the tree line. With that I left that part of my Platoon in that position and moved to join Sgt. Verigan and the other vehicle. I crossed the stream behind him. He had by that time brought the Sheridan on line with his ACAV and was driving up the hill toward the enemy. As he did so, the remaining element of my platoon, under the Platoon Sergeant, stopped firing one by one, so as not to hit our vehicles as we crossed in front of them. As they stopped firing one by one they turned and followed over the stream to join with us. As Verigan's Track and the Sheridan approached the tree line, only the dead and wounded enemy was left on the hill. The rest, very much alive, had gone into the tree line. The Sheridan stopped and fired a flachett round into the enemy. With that, Verigan dismounts his Track and charges into the tree line with a few of his men followed by me, and part of my crew, right behind them.

The shooting was over very quickly as the ferocity and suddenness of our attack had stunned the enemy. We pulled five enemy soldiers out of that tree line; and, the rest had gone to meet their maker. A couple of those captured were female NVA nurses, which we had never seen before. We quickly picked up all the AK-47s that had been scattered about the field and tree line. Pictures were taken of the prisoners with various members of the platoon. As I was walking by the area where we were holding the prisoners, I happened to glance in that direction and I saw one of the male prisoners, a very young man sitting quietly. His arms were tied behind him. Several feet away from him one of my men had put down his M-16 rifle. As I looked at him I had a feeling or premonition that he was going to lunge over and try to somehow pick up that rifle and start shooting. I slowly raised up my rifle and pointed it at him with my finger on the trigger. I looked at him and he looked at me and our eyes met. I read nothing in them, neither fear nor hatred or any emotion at all. I do know that if he had made the slightest movement toward that rifle I would have shot and killed him without hesitancy. After a passage of time, while looking at him, I called out for the trooper who had put his rifle down in the wrong spot to pick it up. He did so and the moment passed.

I called in for helicopter extraction of the enemy wounded and enemy prisoners. At the time I thought nothing of this, but in later years I wondered what happened to them? The ARVIN were not noted for their treatment of enemy prisoners or the conditions under which they were kept. Did they die in captivity, were they tortured, or were they expatriated at the end of the war returning to their families? No way to ever know. The Platoon had operated smoothly, quickly, with maximum efficiency and minimum direction. Each TC, the Platoon Sergeant, the Lead Track Sergeant Verigan, had all followed my directions to the T. Further, they had improvised as necessary using their skills and abilities. We had not only saved the American Infantry unit but had destroyed that enemy unit for the most part. Sergeant Verigan was awarded the Silver Star for his actions that day. Clearly and deservedly earned. I was awarded a Bronze Star with a V devise for valor. I always felt that I had done nothing different than what the men in my platoon had done; and, that the Bronze Star awarded to me, was really given in recognition of their valor and deeds on that day in August 1970. I accepted it and retain it in that spirit. As a sequel to the story, I would note that when we left that hill later that day we left the enemy dead on it unburied. This included a young woman, I assume a nurse, who we had originally placed on a stretcher and who had died before a medivac helicopter could arrive. We never left our dead and the enemy would never leave theirs and would come back to retrieve them. Knowing this we set up Mechanical Ambushes on the paths leading to the area containing their dead. When we came back the next day, one of the Ambushes had gone off killing one more enemy soldier who was lying there with his AK-47 next to him. Their dead from the previous days fight were still there. We took up the enemy weapon, searched his body for documents and left for good this time leaving all their dead in place to be buried, or not, by their comrades.

The separation from Charlie Troop probably only lasted the mission. In hindsight it seems it was longer. At the end of that mission, the CO called me over and said we could rejoin the Troop if I apologized. I told him "No, nothing to apologize for." He said, "Apology accepted and paint your blue back on." Well, we of course did so but as I said it had been a defining moment. It also showed me how deep the trust was that the CO had in 3rd platoon to complete its assigned mission and to care for and safeguard itself while operating alone.

9/10/1970, Grant Coble, My last night in Vietnam was at bar drinking. A band was playing C&W music. The Filipino singer sang like Johnny Cash. At a table in front of the band sat 4 FNG's.

The rest of the bar contained old timers. The pivot man of the 4 decided to throw some ice at the singer who immediately stopped and stared at the punks. They laughed only for a few seconds when they realized that everyone else not only was staring at them but had their hands on their knives. The 4 quickly cowed down into a submissive position, debating among themselves what to do. The bar was dead silent. The first, in a very submissive posture, slunk towards the door and broke into a dead run once within feet of it. The others followed, using the same posture. The rest of the night was quiet.

The next quiet moment was broken with cheers and clapping on the plane as the pilot announced, "You have just crossed the territorial waters of the Republic of South Vietnam." I sat there an wondered if 'It was a cruel dream and I would wake up still there.'

9/23/1970, Carl Wronko, John Bass was a medic assigned to C Troop, 2nd Platoon. I was not there when he died but saw it. Third Platoon had been assigned a separate mission to scout an area in the Pineapple Forest. I had taken 3rd Platoon up on top of a near by hill where we could have a clear field of vision and fire, if it came to that. Second and 1st Platoons remained together with Captain John LaRoche's HQ's element and were tasked with searching a vile. From where 3rd Platoon was situated I could see the 1st and 2nd Platoons approach the vile and begin a dismounted search. I was told later that there were no people in the village but it was occupied with cooking fires lit and personal belongings in the various hooch's. All of a sudden I saw an ugly yellow-brown cloud explode in the middle of the village followed immediately by the sound of an explosion. I turned my radio to the Troop Net and shortly heard a dust-off being called for. Very shortly a dust-off helicopter with the red cross symbol on it's side arrived on the scene and several stretchers were taken up to it and loaded on, followed by the chopper taking off very quickly.

If I recall correctly, there were three troopers wounded. One, whose name I cannot remember, had tripped a mine and had both of his legs blown off. The other two, who were nearby, were wounded by that mine as well. The medic, John Bass had been hit with just one piece of shrapnel, as I was told. It hit him in his chest and entered his heart and killed him very quickly.

9/23/70, John Dabney Bass, Lynchburg, VA, Explosive Device, 7W/84

Anthony John Newman, "Humpty Dumpty's Men,"
To this very day I can pick out that sound,
of that medi-vac bird thumping mercy bound.
To the most difficult L.Z.'s and A.O.'s around,
To pick up the wounded and dead on the ground.

Who knows what they're thinking,
The men in those birds,
Death wings both day and night,
Silent tormenting words.

10/1970, Our area of operations was in a location that was fairly populated. Invariably we would come into contact with the local Vietnamese people, their homes, and their rice fields. That contact did take on different forms. We sometimes stayed outside of a large size town near the Black Ball or Highway 1. This would lead to visits from all sorts of local people. During the day sellers of ice would arrive on their mopeds with the blocks strapped onto the back. Then the negotiation as to price would begin. Ice was valuable stuff and came in blocks of about two and a half feet long. The longer the negotiations went the less 'product' there was to sell, so both sides tried to quickly agree on a price. Once the deal was struck, the representative of each platoon quickly brought the platoon's share to it's AO where the ice was broken up into pieces for each track. Mostly the ice was used to cool cans of soda as you didn't trust to put it into a drink as it contained who knows what kind of life. In addition, young ladies would come and spread out their objects for sale (not talking sex here) but bandanas, peace symbols, neck chains, bananas, and much more. Prices were fixed by bargaining and they were good at it. Later, on toward evening a different group of ladies might appear and they would usually be accompanied by their brother, father, or uncle who would handle the business end of the transaction which usually took place inside of an ACAV with its rear door down and access covered by a poncho liner.

It was at times like these that my shirt became popular. When I was first asked if someone could borrow my shirt, I was perplexed as to what was up. I was enlightened; it seemed the Lt. got free access to the young ladies. So, whoever had the shirt on, got it for free. My shirt did much better than I ever did. There was plenty of action while I did not. Could never bring myself to have an interest in one of the Vietnamese people, perhaps a prejudice, I don't know. Years later at reunions, I would joke with Ron Castor who borrowed my shirt the most, that he had fathered and left in Vietnam many children. His response was that might be true but their last names were all "Wronko" as my name was on my shirt.

We also took up positions outside of small villages as well for purposes of covering a Medcap. Our Medics or Docs and sometimes the real Doc from the Squadron HQ. Would set up besides the road and treat any and all for anything; and , I do mean anything. Sores, infected eyes, maggots in the hair, whatever - these people and their children would have it. While they worked we would sit on and around our tracks and talk to the people and throw or pass out candy or 'chop chop' which was their way of saying food or C Rations. Always attracted a crowd. Mike Sargo would always be in the middle of it. He would have been elected mayor of the area hands down. He'd even been to inside their huts or hutches to visit with them. I remember one family that he pretty much adopted. Whenever we would pass by them, in he would go carrying C Rations, usually the good stuff, with meat, and he'd leave it with them. He said they didn't get meat much and he wanted to help them. I went into their home a few times with him and they seemed to appreciate him and what he was doing but, you simply could not read those people.

I also kept running into a young boy when we stopped near Tam Ky. He must have been about 12 or 13 years old and was very intelligent. I think his family was well off, as he did not look like the product of the rice growing villages in the area. He would talk about what it would be like when the war was over. I tried to explain that we Americans would not be staying after the war ended. We were not like the French who had colonized Vietnam. We were there to help his country secure it's freedom and then our large military presence would be gone. In fact we were already downsizing our forces and turning the war over to the Arvin who was expected with our help to safeguard their own freedom. He had a lot of trouble understanding this and expected us to stay forever. I also expected the out come when Vietnamazation was over, to result eventually in victory for the NVA. When I mentioned this possibility he could not comprehend it. How would we American's let that happen, I must be joking with him. I, of course, was right. I often wondered what happened to him. Did he stay near Tam Ky or become a boat person? If his family were of the upper class and the Saigon Government, his future would not have been too bright. But, given his intelligence, I'd like to think he turned out OK and maybe is even a government functionary in Vietnam today.

We'd next encounter the people in the more remote villages that we would be surrounding and searching. Most of these villages were empty when we drove up by them and got off the tracks and went into them. Lets face it, you'd have to be deaf, dumb, and blind not to hear a Platoon of Armored Vehicles approaching your home. Often, no one there but a cook fire was still burning and personal belongings were all around. If there were people left, they were usually very young or very old. They very rarely spoke, sometimes did not even watch you, unless you started taking something of theirs. Never did we find a male of military age. They were gone in one of the Vietnamese Armies, ARVIN or VC, or they had taken off into the jungle or mountains to avoid service in one or the other. The old women were always a sight; they chewed beetle nut a lot and had rotten old red teeth. If our search turned up something, which could be of aid to the enemy, we destroyed it. An example would be more rice than was thought necessary for one family.

I do remember one time, when we had finished searching a village, we then set up to eat and stay out of the heat of the midday sun, I, Norman "Red" Bourgault, and another guy started walking down a trail leading away from the village we had just searched merely for something to do. We were moving very quiet, no noise at all. I saw a hooch off by itself in the distance and walked slowly over to it with my M-16 in a ready position. I eased my way to the front entrance and looked in and saw a young woman sleeping on a rice mat. I slowly walked in, my rifle ready. I looked around, sow no evidence of anyone else there. Looked over by her and saw no signs of weapons. No signs of children or work being done. Walked back out and looked for the men from my Platoon and did not see anybody. Looked back in, she was still sleeping, no sign at all that she was aware of my presence. Thought it over. What to do? To get my men or not. To have our Kit Carson Scout's interrogate her. Find out who she was. Were her hands those of hard working villager or were they the soft hands of an NVA nurse? An enemy or a villager? Decided to just walk quietly away. I let 'sleeping beauty' continue her rest unmolested. Don't know why; don't know why even after all these years. Maybe by this time in my tour, I wanted someone to not be harmed by this war, I really don't know why. Who knows, being all alone at the time, maybe I was the dumb ass in danger and just didn't know it. Hope she is OK to this day, having raised a fine family and having had a peaceful life.

Kit Carson Scouts. They were former Viet Cong for the most part, and some NVA who had surrendered themselves to our forces with a promise of good treatment. They were offered a chance to be trained and then to serve with American units as guides, translators, and scouts. We had one assigned to our Platoon by the name of Nuie who rode one of the Sheridan Tanks with Steve Rockwell. They were close. Nuie, however, was not much good in any of the roles of a Kit Carson Scout. He liked to stay out of harms way on the tank. Well who could blame him, our war was over in a year and his would go on until one side won. We did have another Kit Carson Scout assigned to our CO be the name of Sgt. Fouk (pronounced by us as Fook). He stayed with the Troop Hq. Unit and he was very, very good. He had been in the NVA, had had his family killed by them as I understand it and was highly motivated in return. His information and familiarity of NVA operations was a lifesaver at times and, at other times, enabled us to bring down a lot of hurt on the enemy. I hope he got out of the country when it fell to the Communists, as I don't think they would have regarded him as a candidate for rehabilitation.

Anthony John Newman, "Marvin,"
Marvin the Arvin,
What a frail sort of folk.
These are our allies,

My God, what a joke!
The best of equipment,
Re-supply and chow.
Did it make any difference?

And where are they now?
When the fighting is thickest,
And every man's a must,
You'll know quite quickly,
That Marv you can't trust.

The fighting is over,
When Marv does appear,
Medi-Vac's are leaving,
He's trying to sell you a beer!

One of our most sought after missions was to guard the town of Tam Ky when its ARVIN Armor unit went out into the field. If my memory serves me well that unit was designated the 3rd Squadron, 4th Armored Regiment and its home base was Tam Ky which it was tasked to protect. It protected the town well, hardly ever leaving it to take the field. When it did have to go out on a mission or an operation, about every month or two, one of our Troops would take its place. We would set up separately, by platoons, just outside of the town on the side facing the mountains where trouble, if it came, would most likely come from. There we would stay for several days while the people of the town came to visit as I described earlier. Tam Ky also contained a CORDS compound. I forget what the words were supposed to mean; but it was for civilian advisers to the South Vietnamese Forces, maybe read CIA here. The compound had a small sized PX where you could purchase wine, liquor and beer of a better vintage than normally available to us. As I recall, it was off limits to enlisted personnel but not to officers. So, I would go shopping with a list provided by the barred EMs and my own desires. It was good duty.

I have two stories of interest to tell here. First, after making my purchases one day, I returned to our Platoon Lager. Much to my surprise, Captain LaRoche was there. He was supposed to have gone on some mission with one of both of the other two platoons. Well he always knew where to go to have a good time. Here I came carrying a bag full of bottles. In response to his questions about what I had, I decided to not evade and escape as I was caught red handed, so to speak, and I replied that I had several bottles o wine which were for dinner and he was invited. He took me up on the offer and extended the invitation to the other platoon leaders and our Forward Artillery Officer who rode on Commander's ACAV. We proceeded to convene the C Troop Officers Mess. I had an ACAV set up with the words "C Troop Officers Mess" sprayed on it with shaving cream. I had a tarp placed so that it extended out from the top of my ACAV providing a tent like roof. We set up a table, don't know where my boys got it from, and put a white parachute over it to serve as a table cloth. We had hot chow that day which was helicoptered in from our mess hall. Captain John LaRoche, C Troop Co; Lt. Richard Forbes, 1st Platoon Leader; Lt' Steve Keller, 2nd Platoon Leader, Lt. Carl Wronko, 3rd Platoon Leader; and, Lt. Glenn Morrell, Forward Artillery Observer all sat down to dinner. The wine was opened and served by Staff Sgt. Earl Verigan, Sgt. Mike Sargo, and his staff from 3rd Platoon, served the dinner. Such was how all my wine came to be consumed. All and all, it was fun and a good time was had by all.

When we were guarding Tam Ky, our state of alertness did suffer and admittedly it should not have since we were in a war zone. We were in the outskirts of the town and there were distractions as I've already set out. One evening, a man on a motorcycle coming from the town itself, drove up to the rear of my platoon and into our logger. He was wearing a set of black pajamas. He rode in a circle behind our tracks and then stopped and got off of his motorcycle. Everyone who was on guard just watched him. He started yelling at everyone and asking for whoever was in charge. I walked up to him with my Platoon Sergeant beside me. He told me that he was from the CORDs compound, that he was retired military, and that our guard was a disaster. He was going to turn me in. He said a proper guard would have challenged him, and not let a man on a motorcycle wearing black pajamas into our position where he could have thrown a satchel charge. He was right. What to do? I turned to Sgt. Thomas and said , "This man is right and our guards should have responded." Sgt. Thomas said, "Lt. - the guy is obviously a white man and my people are not going to shoot a white guy riding a motorcycle up to, and then into our position." The guy stood there with a grin on his face. I looked at him and then I looked at Thomas. "Sgt. Thomas," I said, "This man is absolutely right. Have our guards shoot him now when he gets on his motorcycle. When it's done, let me know and I will report the perceived attack on our position to higher headquarters. When we then find out it was a Caucasian instead of an Asian, I will explain that he came up in the dusk, wearing black pajamas and that an honest mistake was made, as no white man in his right mind would have done this." The guy stopped grinning about half way through my instructions to the Sergeant and jumped on his motorcycle and left. Never heard a thing about it from anybody. Was glad nobody took me serious and shot the man. Then I would have had to do some real explaining, but then he never did report us.

Vietnam was also a different kind of war from a perspective of rules of engagement and operations. There were no front lines behind which you were safe. We operated in Indian Country and when we went to the rear for rest and refitting we were still subject to attack. It could come from any quarter, at any time and any place. A day in the field began with the last guy on watch waking everyone up around sunrise, we would pack our gear onto the tracks, take in any booby traps we had set the night before, roll up the RPG screen and put it on the rear hatch of the ACAV, and eat a breakfast of C Rations. The CO would advise the mission, and off we would go. If it was a Troop sized mission one of the platoons would lead off and be followed by the rest. If it was a platoon mission we would take off on our own. We would lead with an ACAV, followed by a Sheridan, followed by my ACAV and would space out the other

Dragoons

vehicles depending upon number and type so that the last vehicle was always an ACAV. The idea of leading and trailing with an ACAV was to allow for a better sight line resulting from the unobstructed view and the greater number of crewman on the ACAV. It would be hot and humid. It was always hot and humid in Vietnam and being on those metal armored vehicles didn't help at all.

As the day wore on, we would shelter in a tree line or a village, after searching it, and have more C Rations for a lunch. We would then continue on with whatever the mission required. As the day wore on, I'd be asked if we needed anything for re-supply and would place an order if needed. Toward evening, we would pick out a place to logger for the night, pull into a circular formation, put up the RPG screens, set up booby traps as warranted for the area, and get ready for the re-supply helicopter. If we did get re-supplied, we usually got a hot meal in metal containers, exchanging the old empty ones for the new filled ones. That was one of the nicer things than being in the infantry, we did get hot chow and I don't think they did or at least not very often. I'd go to the CO's track and get the mission for the next day, and then come back to the platoon and meet with the Track Commanders to go over it. With darkness, we broke the crew down into two-hour watches, one man was always awake at all times and sometimes, depending upon the area, two were on watch. When morning came, the routine would begin again.

The experience of the Troopers would always influence how we performed our missions and I took great pains to allow the men to use their experience. For instance, Mike Sargo, my second TC loved to play with explosives. We even carried a charge or two on our ACAV which didn't always sit to well when you considered what could happen if we hit a mine or took an RPG. Whenever we had to cross a stream, or what we called a Blue because of the blue line on our maps that marked them, Mike refused to take us across in an area where others had already crossed. He felt, and correctly so, that the enemy would consider those used crossing areas an excellent spot to place a mine. So Mike and the TC of the lead track, together with several gunners to cover them, would dismount and look for a likely new place to cross. Inevitably, it involved blowing down a high stream bank on one or both sides of the stream, When the spot was picked, they'd get their charges, dig them in and blow the new crossing. We'd then cross over. Never in my time in the field did we hit a mine crossing a stream. It was just good common sense and we got in lots of practice with explosives.

Before I leave the topic of explosives, I should mention the use of clamor mines for what we termed Mickey Mouse ambushes. Part way through my tour as 3rd Platoon Leader, we were given training in the setting up of remote clamor mine ambushes by soldiers from another army Division which had developed the system. It basically entailed taking a clamor, a battery, a trip wire with a plastic piece on one end, a cloths-pin with metal clap clips attached to one end of a connector wire and a blasting cap on the other end, and putting it all together on a likely trail or avenue of approach. A clamor mine was a square plastic box, curved slightly with the outward arc of the curve to be placed facing the enemy. The mine was filled with an explosive mixture called C-4 behind a load of BB like pellets. When fired, the pellets would be exploded all over the area to the front of the mine, killing or wounding anyone in front. The ambush was set up by placing the clamor facing the direction desired, putting the blasting cap end of the wire into the firing port and attaching the other end of the wire with the cloths pin to a tree or bush, with the plastic piece of the trip wire between the metal of the clothes pin. The trip wire would be placed across the trail. Attaching the battery to a wire also attached to the clothes pin armed the devise. When someone hit the trip wire, the plastic would be pulled out, the metal on the clothes pin would snap together completing the circuit which would fire the blasting cap and killing or wounding anyone in the kill zone. This was an extremely effective booby trap, which was then new to our area, and the enemy did not know of its use. We would place them out in the evening, after we'd stop for the night, so that it was almost dark and we would not be seen deploying them. I can remember about 7 to 10 enemy soldiers being accounted for in this manner.

I can also remember one incident that I wished had never happened. We had set out a Mickey Mouse ambush along a trail through a rice paddy with a bamboo wood-line behind it. When morning came, the patrol sent out to pick it up, discovered that the battery was gone and the cut wire was still in place to the clamor. The patrol left everything, believing that the clamor had been booby trapped itself, and returned to our Platoon logger. I went back with the patrol to look for myself. I didn't want anyone to go pick it up, as an enemy soldier dug in behind it could have rigged it for command detonation. I didn't want anyone to walk to the side of it or around it suspecting that more booby traps could have been set up there. So, I decided to have a Sheridan Tank button up with the crew inside drive in front of the MM. This way the tank crew would be protected if the thing exploded. I had the crew fire a flachett round into the MM which destroyed it.

C Troop, as did all the Troops of the 1/1 Armored Cavalry, operated independently, I can recall only two occasions as a Platoon Leader where that did not happen. Once, in the fall, a Typhoon was predicted to hit the coast of Vietnam near our area of operation. All three troops were ordered to the same high hill, which was north west of Hawk Hill. We loggered in one large circle, with the Armored Vehicles all buttoned up. Our Troopers got to meet with friends in the other two troops. If I recall correctly, the typhoon never amounted to much and we were together only one day.

The other time we were with another Troop element, was a combat situation. My platoon was operating by itself and was at a distance from the rest of our Troop. We had loggered for the night. A call came in that a platoon from Alpha Troop was pinned down in the middle of a stream crossing and needed help fast. Third Platoon was the nearest American unit. Well, we took down our RPG screens, tossed our stuff in the tracks and took off in the compass direction given. In order to go faster, we turned on our headlights and had flares dropped. Strangest feeling in the world as we always practiced light conservation at night. The enemy would know where we were, you can't hide tanks in the middle of a rice paddy, but why show them exactly where your at. We saw more flares being dropped in the distance. As we came up from behind the platoon from Alpha, I could see an ACAV in the middle of a stream, and the rest of them, four of five, on line by the stream. I dismounted my track and ran over to the platoon leader. He told me that as they started across they were fired on from the woods on the opposite bank and had been fired on continuously since. The ACAV had been abandoned by it's people in the middle of the stream. He was concerned that the enemy might be on it an taking their machine guns and weapons. I told him I'd bring my platoon up on either side of his and add our fire power into the tree line on the opposite side, which we did. We didn't take any fire ourselves but opened up with everything. I think when we came up the NVA had taken off but we cleared those woods big time. When their Troop came up, we left and went back to ours.

The hill where all three Troops loggered during the Typhoon would also present me with a dilemma on an other occasion. My platoon was parked there with a good point of observation. One of my Troopers excitedly called me over. He had spotted some soldiers in NVA uniforms and helmets to the north. I quickly saw them and brought my two tanks up to prepare to take the enemy under long range HE fire. I also called back to a fire mission from the artillery. I was quickly told by my CO that there would be no fire mission and that I could not fire my tank main guns at them for they were not in our AO but an adjacent one belonging to the Marines where we were not cleared to fire. We sat there and watched them walk around a hooch where they seemed to be meeting. Nothing happened to them. I thought about having my tanks fire anyway - I mean they were right there! But, I obeyed my orders and didn't fire. In hindsight not firing was the right thing. Maybe there was a marine platoon working toward them, or observing them, and would have fired into the marines. Then again, maybe the bastards knew they were on the boundary of two AOs and knew they would be safe there. This was one of the frustrating times.

Being an effective Platoon Leader required an ability to learn from experience, which entailed both good and bad lessons. Third Platoon was operating independently one day and we loggered on a slightly elevated slope to act as a blocking force and to observe for movement in the surrounding area. Suddenly we were taking mortar rounds, which were landing just outside of our perimeter. I had the tracks button up, crank up, and move from the area. So far so good, but it really ticked me off that we had been fired on and I wanted to fire back at whoever had mortared us. I remembered my OCS training at this point. We had been instructed during a class on mortars that they make a 'splash' indentation on the ground when they explode whereby the force of the blast creates a sort of T shaped indentation, with the cross of the T in front of you and the leg of the T pointing away. To tell where the mortar fire was coming from you simply went to where the mortars had landed and, standing parallel to the 'cross of the T'; you lined up the leg of the T with your compass and shot a reverse direction. So I took my ACAV back to where the mortars had landed, got out, went up to the mortar 'splash', shot a reverse direction and marked it off on my map. With that I drove back to the rest of the platoon an called over my mortar track TC and gave him the direction to fire. As far as distance went, I looked on the map and figured out what I thought would be 'likely' places to have fired from and gave him those. He proceeded to fire the mission.

I reported to the Troop Commander that we had taken mortar fire and had returned it; that we had no casualties and none were known as to the enemy. The guys in the platoon thought all this was just great getting back at Charlie. However, in hindsight, I'd not have done it. When we went back to where the mortars had landed, the target area, who was to say that a few more mortars could have been fired into that same area only this time with me and a few of my crew out in the open. Further, by shooting the reverse direction for an unknown distance, I could have dropped our mortars on 'friendly' positions; and who knows, maybe the mortar fire was just 'harassment' fire from an American or Arvin unit who did not know we were there; and, I just succeeded in firing on one of our own units. Another lesson learned by experience but with no one hurt.

As my time as Platoon Leader progressed there were several instances that stand out. One in particular, I am sure, was unusual for an Armored Lieutenant, but I had been commissioned through Infantry OCS and gone through extensive training in infantry tactics at Ft. Benning and again at Ft. Sherman in the Panama Canal Zone. As a result of this background and training, I was selected to command a combat assault by helicopter with the 'infantry' for the assault make up from members of C Troop. I am not sure how the idea for the plan came about. I am fairly sure that my Troop

Commander, John LaRoche knew of my infantry training; and, maybe, the Squadron Commander did as well.

In any event, the plan I was presented called for me to participate in a helicopter assault with about twelve men. We were to establish a 'blocking' position upon landing. The idea was that the rest of the Troop would drive through an area causing the enemy to flee before them and into our 'blocking position.' Once driven against our position, we could engage them and either destroy them ourselves or hold them until the Troop came up who would engage them as well. Nice plan and if it worked, I was told we would do it again in the future. However none of the Trooper that I was given to make the assault had ever done this before, nor had they operated as pure infantry before. I think I was given about one or two days notice of the plan, so that was all the time I had to train my force.

Since the drivers and TCs and at least one of the gunners had to stay with the tracks, this left me with a force made up of gunners and spare men from different tracks from the separate platoons. Not only had they never done this before, but also they had never worked with each other being from different platoons and tracks. I began to train them. I first had to go over how to prepare to get into the helicopters. I broke them into a group of six per helicopter; and , then broke that group into teams of 3 with a team on either side of the area where the chopper would land. This way 3 of them would board the chopper from each side, getting the 6 of them on quickly. We ran through pretending how to do this several times without benefit of the choppers being there for the practice. Once that was set, we went over how to dismount from the helicopters, again with 3 getting off of each side. I then explained that the helicopters would land with one in front an the second behind it.

In order to protect our landing area, I had them practice dismounting and the troopers from the first chopper running out a few yards and hitting the ground in a semi-circle. Three from the left side going to the 9 o'clock through 12 o'clock position; three from the right side going to the 12 o'clock to the 3 o'clock position. The Troopers exiting the rear chopper would cover the 3 o'clock to 6 o'clock and the 6 to 9 o'clock positions respectively from their left an right dismount. We did this over and over. Line up to jump on, then dismount and take covering positions. While we did not work with actual helicopters on this drill, I think they got enough to know what to expect would happen.

Then I went over what to do after the choppers took off and we were sure the landing was not opposed. This entailed the Trooper in the 12 o'clock position walking forward toward the object in the point position with the Troopers from the various clock directions falling in behind in line. I had to go over spacing of the patrol so that one round or one mortar or booby trap would not get more than one of us; and, to keep quiet and use hand signals only, which was new to them. Normally a track makes so much noise there is no point in being very quiet when you get off them and search an area as the enemy, if there, would know you were there. This went ok as they were used to patrolling away from the tracks for short distances.

Next, when we got to the blocking position, I went over how to go into a line facing the area the enemy would expect to come from, and how to also leave a security element facing the rear and to the sides in case we were approached from those areas. Well, we were as ready as we could be. I had them prepared to carry lots of ammunition, no back packs, water and one c-ration meal. I wanted them light, as they had to march a good way to the blocking position and it would be during the hottest part of the day. I could do nothing for the radio men or those carrying an M-60 machine gun. They would have to just hump it.

Well the big day came, we gathered together and I checked over their equipment and it was fine. We went out to the pick up zone and sat in the shade until we were told the choppers were on approach. We went into the pick up position, the choppers landed, and we all got on. Looked good so far. As we flew to the landing zone we could see helicopter gunships firing up the landing area. I gave the signal to lock and load weapons as we started down. When we hit the ground, everyone dismounted OK an took up the correct positions in the defensive circle for the most part. Thank God it was a cold LZ without any enemy opposition. I often wondered what the helicopters crew's thought of us - they were used to working with real infantry.

Grant Coble

Anyway, it came time to move. This did not go as well as planned. Guys got up an milled around and I had to get about and put everyone in line and tell the point where to head. Once done, we started out. Quiet and stealthy we were not. They moved at a quick pace. I had to slow things down and stop the bunching up and suggest the point man look carefully so he might not walk into an ambush. Again, they were not used to or conditioned for this type of patrol. Reading my map and using my compass, we headed in the right direction. We did find the old abandoned village where we were to set up.

By this time, they were tired, hot, and had used up most, it not all, of their water. I got them in a position where most were facing where the enemy might approach us from and also got out rear and side security. I tried to get them to take cover so they would not be seen, to not move or attract attention, and to be quiet. Some started to fall asleep from the exertion and some wanted to go look for water. We did not enter the position in a manner so as to be unseen for sure.

It was the longest 2 hours or so I ever spent. I truly hoped that no enemy soldiers were 'driven into us', as I had no idea how my armor crewmen would react to an infantry style fight. Actually, I did have an idea and it wasn't comforting. They performed well the mission they were trained for but this was not their element. The best sound I heard all day was that of the C Troop tracks coming up to our position where we rejoined them. After the exercise was over, I had a talk with the CO about the experience and I am glad to say that we never undertook this maneuver again.

In their element our Troopers were excellent. Here is an example; we were alerted for a mission, which might entail taking on a dug in enemy battalion. A captured VC told our intelligence section that an entire NVA battalion was located to the west of our normal area of operations. The Troop proceeded, with 3rd Platoon leading the way, to the site. Once there I gave the order and the tracks went on line and stopped, facing the wood line. We were in flack jackets and were locked and loaded ready to advance into them. It was at times like these that you felt the fear in your stomach. Anyone who says they had no fear in them at times like this is a liar. I often thought it was easier for me as I had to give the orders, ready the Platoon to launch our attack and then issue more orders as the attack proceeded. It kept my mind busy and I at least knew what was happening and when it was to happen. The individual soldier on the tracks did not have that luxury. The orders came and I directed 3rd Platoon to advance and the Sheridans and ACAVs began to go forward at a steady pace.

As we approached the wood line, I gave the command to open fire and we did, while continuing to move forward together, each track covering the other. Each man working smoothly, firing, refreshing ammo supplies, driving steadily on. No return fire came. No NVA battalion was there and maybe had never been there but we did not know that as we went in. We kept the tracks on line, surrounding the area and began to search it looking for signs of the enemy. Someone found a hole in the ground. It was a small entrance to a tunnel. We went to work on it, throwing colored smoke grenades and CS grenades into that hole. Others of us did not watch the work but rather kept their eyes on the surrounding terrain. Sure enough, our colored smoke began to come out of other hidden holes, which were quickly guarded. None of us wanted to go down into that tunnel and I was not about to order anyone to do what I didn't want to do personally.

We began to seal the many holes by blasting them with charges. As we did so, two VC or NVA came out of one of the holes and were taken prisoner. This was the NVA battalion. I often thought that one disgruntled VC had deserted because he was angered at something one of his comrades had done to him and he then gave away their position to us to gain his revenge, which led to the 'intelligence coup' we had gotten. If so, he'd gotten his revenge on the two who came up. But, that was all we had found and if there were others in the tunnels they either were buried in them or knew of another way out, which was most likely the case.

When this day was over, and we had loggered for the night, one of my Track Commanders came over to me and asked to talk. We had received some new men who had just arrived in country before this incident. The TC told me that one of the guys who was newly assigned to his track had laid down to hide on the floor of the ACAV and did not fire his machine gun no matter what the TC threatened him with. This was a serious matter. If we had been in a combat situation the key would be to gain fire superiority over the enemy, put out more rounds than he did, thus forcing him to take cover so we could safely ride right up to him and either kill him or cause him to surrender. One man not firing means less rounds going out which endangers the rest of the crew. What to do? If he was a coward, then the others would not accept him into their crew and he would be in danger from them as well. They certainly would do nothing to protect or help him if they believed him to be an endangerment to themselves. I told the TC to have the man report to me. When he came over, the fear in him was still showing and he was obviously at a loss as to what to do in his situation.

I had him walk away from my crew with me so we could talk in private. I told him what the TC had told me and asked him what happened. All he could say was he was so scared that he just fell down and couldn't get back up. He didn't want to do this but he could not help it. It was his first time and he had no idea what was going to happen. I let him talk on. When he was done, I spoke softly to him so that he would listen carefully to my words. I told him he was assigned to 3rd Platoon for his entire tour and he would stay there. That an ACAV crew fought as a team, that each depended upon the other for survival and protection; and , if he expected that from the others in the crew, they had to know they could count on the same from him in return. I told him to concentrate on and focus on the machine gun that he was assigned to; and, to listen to the others who had been in country a lot longer and knew much which would help him to get home alive. I also pointed out that the bottom of an ACAV was no place to hide as the floor was covered with boxes of ammunition; that the storage areas had explosives in them; and, that one RPG round through the side of the ACAV would set all that off and kill him in an instant. I also pointed out that if the Track ran over a mine and he was laying on the bottom of it that he would be killed out right as well, which is why the men rode on top of the ACAVs. I suggested he overcome his fear, that it was natural to be afraid, but that if he expected to get home alive that he'd better stay off the bottom of the ACAV where death surely awaited him.

He understood also that he would not be getting out of the field until his year was up. When I finished he still didn't look too solid and I did not have any way of knowing if our talk had done any good; and wouldn't until the next time we faced a combat situation. When we got back to my Track I sent him back to his and told him to send his TC over to me.

I went over with the TC what I had said and done and asked to be informed as to how he performed in the future. If he could not conquer his fears, I would get him off that Track before he affected the ability of the rest of the crew. Obviously, we didn't shoot cowards during this time though I never even mentioned the possibility to him; but if it kept up he would have to go.

I wish I could recall what happened with him after but I don't, which leads me to think he worked out OK. I think I would remember it if he had done it again and had been removed. Frankly, I don't even remember his name, which is just as well.

10/1970, I recall another man I had to deal with who I believe was an absolute coward. He was a shake and bake Sergeant which means he went through Sergeant School back in the States after he finished his Advanced Training and was though to be leadership material. This man, whose name I do recall but will not mention, came to me as an E-5 or Three Stripe Sergeant, near the end of my tour as 3rd Platoon Leader. Given his rank, I assigned him as a TC to an ACAV. After a while it became obvious that he was never going to the field as his Track was constantly breaking down immediately after repairs when it left to join us on a mission. In accordance with Squadron policy when a track broke down it and it's entire crew would be hauled back to our base camp by a recovery vehicle while the rest of the Platoon went on its mission to the field. I began to suspect that he and his crew were sabotaging this track on purpose. This had serious consequences to the rest of the Platoon. It meant one ACAV with its firepower missing from the Platoon for the mission. We had in theory seven ACAVs and 3 Seridans in the Platoon. In actuality we never had that many in the field for various reasons. I usually had two Sheridans and four or five ACAVs at any one time. The loss of that one ACAV endangered the rest of the Platoon especially since 3rd Platoon often operated alone. It was not fair to the mission but more importantly it was not fair to the other men in the Platoon to have to carry the extra weight, so to speak, alone; and, it placed them, by the loss of that extra firepower, in a more dangerous situation. I resolved to do something about it.

The next time the Sergeant's ACAV started out on a mission with us, it again broke down after traveling only a few miles. When I pulled the Platoon over, I got off my ACAV and walked back to the Track. The Sergeant had gotten off and was looking into the engine compartment. When I came up to him, I asked what had happened, and he replied that he didn't know but thought it had something to do with the transmission. I told him flat out that I thought it had to do with something that he and his crew had done to the ACAV. He turned on me and started yelling that I was accusing him of doing it on purpose and he wasn't going to stand for that. I told him that he had it exactly right and we went back an forth yelling at each other. Finally, he said that I was wrong, that there was nothing I could do about it, that the track could not go on the mission and had to go back to Hawk Hill. I told him that he did not have it quite right. With that, I ordered the crew off the ACAV and assigned each one of them to a different ACAV to ride on as an extra crewman. They were going to the field after all. I sent the Sergeant back with the Track to the rear area. I had reasons for this, as I wanted to break the link he had with his crew.

That evening after we had loggered, I had each of his crew sent over to me. I told them I knew what was going on and that the fun was over. I told them that each time that ACAV broke down that they would be going to the field anyway, but not the Sergeant. He would stay with the Track while they went to the field as extras which meant they would join all the dismounted missions as riflemen, they would search the villages (risking booby traps); they would walk the ground (risking stepping on mines); and they would ride on the most exposed part of the ACAV - the area with out gun-shields to protect the gunners and TC. I really didn't have to tell them this. They knew it. It had the affect I wanted.

When that mission was over and that crew went back to their Track there were no more mechanical problems. The crew would not follow the Sergeant's lead because they knew he would not be

Dragoons

the one in danger if it broke down again, they would. The Sergeant's fears never changed however. He went to the field, hardly ever got off the ACAV, and then only to stay around the Track. He had a young wife he had left behind and a young child. But, he was not the only one, and he was in a leadership position where I expected him to perform in a manner so as to save his crew, as well as his own butt.

A side thought, did I risk being fragged by him and this crew. Perhaps so, but I knew the rest of the Platoon supported me and that his crew in their hearts knew I was right and that I was looking out for the best of each and every Trooper in 3rd Platoon. Besides, I was sure and am sure to this day that the man was a coward and didn't think he'd have the guts to even try it. I believe I am and was right about him. I also knew I had to get rid of him before he infected the rest of my platoon.

The opportunity came. Outside of Hawk Hill, was an outpost called OP 10. OP 10 was located on a hilltop and it was just what its name implies, an outpost to interfere with the enemy's approach to our Squadron's rear base area at Hawk Hill. The OP was manned by a platoon of Arvin Soldiers and several Americans. It was surrounded by barbed wire, had bunkers in which to sleep and fight from. The American Sergeant then on the hill was going home an the Squadron Headquarters was looking for a replacement. I had just the man for them. I asked him if he wanted the job; an , to my surprise, he said yes in a very affirmative manner. I told him the job was his and sent him happily on his way to Squadron HQ. He was getting out of the field or so he thought. What I didn't tell him was that one of my Troopers who had spent some time there, had told me it was the scariest place he had ever been assigned. One night the enemy probed them. When they went to fire their mortars in response, they found out that some one had put dirt down the barrels so that the firing pins were covered and the rounds did not fire. Obviously, one or more of the Arvin were actually VC. He told me he was deathly afraid of some of the Arvin turning on them should the hill ever come under attack.

I can only imagine the Sergeant's reaction when he discovered what he had truly gotten himself in for. I admit to a certain amount of guilt pangs about this as I knew where I was sending him; but I believed it made a safer environment for the rest of my Platoon without him in it. Their lives were more important to me than his; and, by his actions, he had made it clear that he only cared about himself and not the men assigned to him. They were better off without him.

I never learned what happened to him after that but for the sake of his family I do hope he made it home in one piece. It was not my intention to cause him any harm but to get him away from us before he caused harm to any of mine.

10/1970, Square Lake. I still remember it but not one member of my unit recalls it. The French had constructed the lake, or so I was told, and it was square in dimension and large in size. I was told that the area around it was heavily mined and it was a place to be avoided. A track or tank from Alpha Troop had run over a mine there and had been obliterated. When the Alpha Troop commander had gotten off of his track to help evacuate the wounded and assess the situation, he stepped on another mine and was killed outright. I was told, but don't know if any of this is true or not, that his family was Catholic and that they donated money to the local Catholic Vietnamese orphanage in Tam Ky in the name of their deceased son.

So we were to operate in the area of Square Lake; and, as usual, Cpt. LaRoche had Third Platoon running lead. He told me to be very careful in charting our course to stay away from the Square Lake area as we moved through. Map in hand I began to do just that.

One problem in navigation through that area is that the terrain features surrounding you are all the same. You need to look to the mountains in the far distance and pick out clear features to navigate by. Must have gotten my features in the distance mixed up, for next I knew my lead track came up to a berm and proceeded up it, with the Sheridan Tank behind it followed by the C-36 Track. What I saw when we reached the tip was that we were atop the berm surrounding Square Lake which was spread out before me. Called up the CO on the radio and told him I had Square Lake in sight. He told me to make sure I stayed away from it and was not to pleased when I told him I was 'on top of it.' We were unable to back down or turn around, so I proceeded to travel down one side of the berm with the whole Troop following to the next corner of the square and then down that side to the base.

As we crossed the area adjacent to it in departing the immediate area I saw small remnants of a blown up armored vehicle. If you could hear a pin drop on a moving armored vehicle as we went by that area, it was that quiet. I sat lightly on my seat. Thank God the mines were long gone because our units had never operated there after the Alpha Troop incident or they had rusted away in the wet climate. Thought he never said anything about it, I wondered if the CO would have as much faith in my map reading skills again. In any event we stayed lead platoon so my question was answered.

On a few occasions, we operated in searching an area with Helicopter scout ships. They would travel ahead of us and would look for enemy soldiers. The idea being that they could spot them before the noise of our armor moving toward them clued them to our approach.

One day this approach was successful. The Helicopters started radioing to us that they had spotted some VC moving through an area ahead. The choppers started firing into the bushy area where they had made their sighting and we drove up to it and added our fire to theirs. The bushy growth was too thick to drive an armored vehicle through so the CO had each platoon dismount a ground force which was directed to move into the thick shrubs and to search for and close with the enemy.

As I have said before, most of my troopers were not infantry trained so I did not feel right in having one of them walk point. I took up the point position and started leading in the troopers from 3rd platoon who followed me single file. As we came to a particularly thick area the trail I was following took a sharp bend to the right and I stopped and lay down to figure out how to move up to and through it.

Next I heard an M-16 fire from up ahead and around the bend, followed by shouting "I got one of them." With that I got up and quickly moved around that bend in the trail. What I saw before me was a dead VC who had just been shot by Roberto Arce from 2nd

Platoon. Roberto had gotten separated from his platoon and had gone off on his own as I recall it. In moving through the shrubbery, Roberto had come upon a VC who was lying down and facing in the direction I was approaching from and immediately shot him with his M-16. In the dead VCs hand was a Chi-com grenade. If RC had not come upon that VC, I had no doubt who that grenade would have been meant for. I owed my physical well being and maybe my life to RC. That VC had been left behind to slow or stop our pursuit of the others with him. Even though he had not had the time to throw the grenade, it worked as we stopped and went no further into the bush. The other VC owed their lives, and maybe some of my troopers as well should we have gotten up to the main group and started a firefight, to the VC who had stayed behind and given his life for his comrades. These enemy soldiers were not lacking in courage or dedication to their fellow soldiers.

If I had been wounded I would have been in good hands. Our platoon medic at the time was Hector Garza. Hector was a young Mexican kid from Texas and would prove his courage and abilities many times in the future. Hector rode the C-36 track with my crew and me. When he first joined 3rd platoon he was all fired up to go at the enemy and we had to come to an understanding. We got to that understanding real fast after his first mission with us.

We had stopped outside of a ville to search it, which we did with out discovering anything. I had returned to my track and was sitting on top of it when Hector called up to me and said he had found a hole. I looked down to him as he was just standing next to my side of the C-36 track. He is standing there with a grenade in his hand and proceeds to toss it into a 'hole' in a paddy dike that we were parked next to. In the time it took for my brain to register what he was doing, I rolled off my seat and into the interior of the ACAV landing with a heavy thud on top of our stored ammunition cans.

Silence. No explosion. I waited a few moments and then got up and climbed off the opposite side of the track. The hole that he had 'fragged' was no deeper than a foot or so. If that grenade had exploded, the opening in the hole would have directed the force of the explosion and it's shrapnel right at my track and yours truly. Now I was not in a happy mood. A look into the hole revealed the grenade sitting there with its safety band still on. The inexperienced medic had pulled the pin prior to throwing it but he had forgotten to release the safety catch that kept the 'spoon' of the grenade from flying off and arming it.

Needless to say Hector and I had a little 'talk' about the function of a medic in an Armored Cav. Platoon, as I explained it was not his job to create casualties but to care for them. He was to leave the combat to the combat soldiers. We had no more problems. Hector Garza, after I got out of the field, would earn the Bronze Star when a 3rd Platoon track, C-32 hit a mine. The blast threw the crew riding on top of the ACAV clear as it flipped the track onto its side, trapping the driver. Hector ran up to it, threw open the ear door and, in complete disregard for his own safety, climbed inside the track which was filled with ammunition and various explosives that could explode at any time from the mine blast. He made his way through the torn up track and freed the trapped driver, pulled him out and administered first aid to his wounds and those of the rest of the crew.

The driver had been holding onto the steering levers and the force o the explosion had torn off some of his fingers. Hector was not about to lose one of 'his boys' if he could do anything about it.

I mentioned the use of Rocket Propelled Grenades before. The primary anti-tank weapon that the NVA an VC had was the RPG. It was a conical shaped charge at the end of a round 'stick.' It was shoulder fired with an aiming sight on it. When it hit an object such as a tank or bunker and exploded, a single stream of hot gases shot forward and burned a hole into the target where the force of the explosion was greatly magnified. I only saw one track that had been hit by an RPG. It had a small hole where it had impacted the ACAV and a small hole on the inside. Looking at it, it was hard to believe that such a little 'hole' could do so much damage.

The only time one was fired at us when I was in the field was at the end of day's mission of uneventful patrolling an area. My platoon was leading the way into a nighttime logger. We had just started circling the first few tracks when I heard two loud explosions to my rear. Looking back over my shoulder, I saw that a Sheridan Tank in one of the other platoons had been fired at with two RPGs.

Neither had hit it, but had passed just to the rear of it and exploded on the ground beyond.

The fire had come from the adjacent wood line where you could see the smoke and bushes moving from the back blast of the RPGs. Neither of the two platoons reacted at all. Quite strange. They just kept going along heading toward the logger I was establishing. Most of my platoon was in the logger and our part of the arc that had been set up was facing the wood line. I started firing my M-16 at the area, had my Mortar Track put rounds to the rear of it expecting that the NVA or VC would have taken off to their rear, and had my tracks charge straight ahead toward the wood line. We were firing our 50 caliber and M-60 machine guns toward the wood line as we went. We took no fire as we approached and entered the wood line, which was quite thick. I led a dismounted patrol into the area and found nothing. There had to be at least two of them but they were gone. We looked for a trail of some sort but there was none.

When we got back to the Troop area the CO was 'speaking' to the other platoon leaders about the lack of response to the attack. Fearing more RPG attacks, he decided that the area selected for the night logger was to close to the wood line on one side and a small gorge on the other. I led off to a more open area. By this time, it was dark and he called for the artillery to fire illumination rounds just ahead of us as we moved to the new area so we could see the way to the new position. I recall the sound of those shells exploding over our heads and the whirl of the artillery casings as they fell around us. Kept thinking, 'great the RPGs missed us but now were are going to get hit by our own casing's but we were fine.

10/1970 to 3/1971, Robert Nuccitelli, Captain, Troop Commander

11/1970, One of my last missions in the field was Squadron wide. The Squadron was tasked to go up north of our normal area of operations to protect the rice harvest from interruption by the VC. This would take us into a Marine area of operations. I remember Captain Robert Nuccitelli calling myself and the other platoon leaders into his hooch on Hawk Hill to be prepped on the movement after he had met with the Colonel. He was new to the command of C Troop, having replaced John LaRoche shortly before this. Charlie

Troop was to lead the other two Troops into the area. The Colonel had specifically required this and also that 3rd Platoon lead the way for Charlie Troop. No surprise in this for me since we had been doing it for quite a while now on the Troop level.

When we moved out I was in direct radio contact with the Squadron Commander who controlled our movement. We proceeded north up Highway 1, which was paved. As we came to an area where there was a Vietnamese village with rice fields surrounding it, the Colonel directed me to turn left and head toward the mountains. There was a dirt road there but instinct being what it had become; I had my platoon make the turn off the road and into a rice paddy, which was flooded with rice in full growth. Needless to say the effect on the rice crop as we tracked through that field, as well as the succeeding ones, and over the built up dikes between them was messy. The dikes themselves were fully breached. But, I knew there were no mines in the cultivated rice fields while there may have been some on that dirt road. The rest of C Troop followed, as did the other two troops in the squadron.

I remember some American Marines came out of the village and just watched us passing over those rice fields. They were assigned to the village as part of a Marine Civil Action Program; and, they lived in it protecting the villagers around the clock. The Marine program (called CAP) was designed to deny access of the village to the enemy and to aid the villagers in their crop production. Thus winning their trust and loyalty. Looking back on it over the years, I don't suppose my decision to flatten those rice fields and the connecting dikes did much to enhance that program.

Sad to say, we just didn't care. But we knew our forces were being removed, no one wanted to die or be wounded in a lost cause, and we had all the faith in the world that the ARVIN would lose to the NVA in a most expeditious fashion. So why risk our lives and well being for those villagers? Anyway, we proceeded across those rice fields and kept going until we came to an area further in which was primarily scrub land. It was good tank country as you could see for a great distance.

We came to a streambed; I got off my ACAV and scouted a route across with Sgt. Jim Dean who was now my lead track commander.

Colonel called for me on the radio and I had to go back to speak with him in my ACAV. He wanted to know what I was doing on the ground and I told him that I couldn't find a way across sitting on my ass on top of the track. In any event, Jim found a likely looking area and he proceeded across while I put tracks out on our flanks to cover the crossing. As Jim's ACAV went up the opposite bank, I sent over another ACAV so they could take up a defensive position so that the rest of the Platoon could cross over. As I recall, it was a fairly step bank and it was a job getting each successive track up it as it got wetter from use.

Once my platoon got across, we picked up our forward movement leaving the area for the succeeding platoons and Troops to get over. As we went on, we came across a destroyed tank that appeared to not be one of ours. I was told later that it was a French Tank that had been there for years since their war in Vietnam. Not much left of it, and our troops sobered a bit as we went by it. I'm glad to say that from then on out it was a quiet mission.

The area was sandy and brushy with not many locations to hide in. If the VC were trying to get through us to the area where the rice was being harvested, we did see some suspicious movement in the higher elevations of the foothills of the mountains and I did call in for a Cobra Helicopter strike. It looked like the possibility of enemy mortar pits being set up. The strike was fun to watch when they came on station. I spoke to the pilots on the radio and directed them and their fire to the suspected area. They worked the area over good and we believe we saw some secondary explosions but could not reach the heights to verify anything.

When the mission was completed and the rice harvest over, we were directed over another dirt road out of the area that linked up with Highway 1. As I recall, 3rd Platoon did not lead that movement out of the area but we were concerned about going over that dirt road. The concern did not last for long. As we passed over the road going out we came upon a Korean Army Armored Unit coming the other way on the road. We were passing through a Korean area of operations and it was quite safe.

Those boys were not restricted in their rules of engagement with the enemy and had been running a virtual reign of terror in their area, or so we were told. As a result of their methods of operation, The VC and NVA gave them a wide berth. I had heard stories about how the Koreans, highly trained in Asian Martial Arts, would go out on patrols where they had killed enemy soldiers with their bare hands while taking no prisoners. Looked like a tough bunch to me and as we passed along side them I thought it was very nice to have them on our side.

11/14/1970, Charles Henry Adams, Thomasville, GA, Drowned, 6W/58

11/15/1970, I leave 3rd Platoon and become Troop Executive Officer (XO), A field soldier in Vietnam looked forward to two things, first was to get out of the field and into a rear job at some point in his tour and then to going home. I was no different. The Army's approach to field assignments for Officers was different than with enlisted men. An enlisted man could expect to spend his entire one-year tour in the field unless he got lucky and was given a rear job. An Officer in a company grade position could expect to spend six months in the field and six months in rear job.

As I approached five months as 3rd Platoon Leader I was now the longest serving Platoon Leader in Charlie Troop. Our Executive Officer at the time had never served in the field; and, frankly I didn't think he could cut it. But he wasn't exactly doing a bang up job as XO either and the Troop Commander was having problems with the rear getting re supplied. I was not above letting him know that I could handle the job and that my expected time in the field was nearing an end. I was happy to learn that I would be the new Troop XO as soon as my replacement was found and broken in.

I spread my news to my platoon. I also made some commitments to some of them that I would end rear positions for them and get them out of the field with me. In a bit, a helicopter landed and a new LT got off. He was West Point and already a First Lieutenant. I remained as Platoon Leader and for several days he rode with me as an observer watching me and listening to my advice. It became quickly apparent that he neither required nor wanted my help or guidance. It was also clear to me that he would not listen to anyone or learn from the experience of others as I had done. He was his own man and that's how it would have to be. I tried to show him how to read a map and how to direct the lead track. Declined the offer, he knew what to do and thank you.

On his second day, we were operating alone and a sniper started firing rounds from a nearby wood line at us. One went very near to me and I still recall the cracking sound as it went by. He put the platoon on line and was about to give the order to open fire with the Tank main guns and all the machine guns.

I stopped him and asked him if he knew where he was on the map and where the other platoons and HQ. tracks were? He said he did and pointed it out to me. I told him he was wrong, that he was being set up by the VC to fire at a wood line, which masked our other platoons. In other words he was about to fire on our own Troop.

He insisted I was wrong and that he was right. In hindsight, I can see that I was embarrassing him in front of my command track crew, which was in the process of becoming his crew.

The event would quickly circulate to the entire platoon and troop. I took the radio hand set from him and called the CO and asked him to shoot a flare up in the air at his position. He did so. We sat there quietly as the flare rose up from behind the wood line we were facing and which he was about to unload every weapon we had into.

That evening I went over to speak with the CO. He asked me if my replacement was ready to go it alone. Nice position to be in. If I tell it as it is I may lose or delay my chance to be XO. If I pass on him, I'll be out of the field but my Platoon would be left in the care of this loser. I told the CO what I thought of him and about the reason for the flare. How could I do otherwise? The CO said nothing and I went back to 3rd Platoon.

The next day I was told to take the re-supply chopper back to the rear and assume my duty as XO. I did so but no longer gladly with the happiness of leaving the field in my heart. I wish I could say the story had a happy ending and that my replacement turned out all right in the end but it did not happen that way.

Shortly after assuming command, he took the platoon right down the middle of a bowling ally and the lead track, C-32, hit a mine and flipped over on it's side. This is the event gone over earlier where Hecto Garza, the medic of Doc, earned the Bronze Star. It was really hard for me to take when I learned what had happened. My replacement was relieved of his command shortly after this.

I was left with a guilt trip and the belief that I had stayed with my platoon that this would not have happened. Instead of looking out for my own well being, I should have stayed with my platoon and looked after the well being of my men. Thirty years later I still wrestle with that problem and my choice, to the extent I had one. I wasn't going to make a career out of the Army; I was a good platoon leader and didn't need to get my ticket punched on the way to a promotion. I acknowledge that I probably would have had no choice in the matter anyway as it was the Army's policy that I go to the rear after a six-month tour in field command. But now I think I could at least have tried.

12/7/1970, David Pitmon, The unit returned from a mission, but then went back out, working the same area in the Pineapple Forest. We used some of the same loggers sites used during the previous mission. The old timers said not to use the same areas but went unheard. Pulling into one old logger a tank hit a Bouncing Betty mine which stopped the tank. Several soldiers got off their tracks and went to see what damage had been done as did Joe Crenshaw and Tom Lafferty. Lafferty was the Platoon Sniper, but had yet to receive his M-14 with scope. He had just transferred into the unit. Crenshaw drove the Demo track (APC loaded with demolition charges).

Joe sat down onto the Bouncing Betty mine unwittingly, arming the device. When he went to get up, the Bouncing Betty exploded up form the ground and blew. The blast killed Crenshaw out right and seriously wounded Lafferty. Bill McNabb was hit in the shoulder and I was hit all over the body with shrapnel. When I fell to the ground I landed next to another Betty. You could recognize these by the 3 prongs sticking out of the ground. The entire area was booby trapped. There were about 14 or 15 of us either laying on the ground or wounded. The other troopers used knives and probed the ground clearing paths to us.

The mission was called off as so many of us had been hit. Tom Lafferty died of his wounds as did Carmine Macedonio.

12/7/1970, Joe Edward Crenshaw, Mobile, AL, Landmine, **6W/112**

12/7/1970, Carmine Angelo Macedonio, Williston Park, NY, Landmine, **6W/113**

12/7/1970, Thomas Lee Lafferty, Adrian, MI, Landmine, **6W/113**

1971

1971, LTC Sheldon Burnett, Squadron Commander

1/71 George V Robbins, Chu Lai, Khe Sanh, Da Nang, I would like to take this time and dedicate this story and accounts to all those that gave up their lives so others may live in freedom and other fellow troopers that gave their youth, time, support, and innocence to themselves, United States army, fellow troopers, and the United States of America.

My name is George V. Robbins and this story is about my time with Charlie Troop, 1st Squadron 1st Cavalry assigned to the Americal Division in February of 1971.

Well it all started when I was discharged from the Army in October of 1970 from Viet-Nam. I served in Viet Nam for 2 ½ years and I had a total of 7 ½ years in the military. I made E-5 3 or 4 times and I wasn't getting nowhere in this mans Army. So I decided to go ahead and get out and try to get a job. I went home and from October to January 1971 I could not find a job that would pay me at least what the Army was giving me ($500.00) a month plus. Being in the Army and having served in Viet Nam was not a cool thing at that time. I called the Army Recruiter and asked if there was some way I could come back into the Army without going through Basic Training again. The recruiter told me that they had this program that if you were out of the military less than 18 months you could come back into the military without going through training and you would be able to keep your same rank that you got out with. You just would lose your time in grade. Now that sounded like a deal to me. So in I went.

1/27/,1971, I went back in and requested to go back to Viet Nam (3rd tour) ASAP. Well, they put a new meaning to the word ASAP. February 4th (7 days) I was in Viet Nam in Chu Lai Combat Center, Americal Division. The Combat Center was designed to give the new soldier a heads up on what to expect in Vietnam, so I stayed there, oh, for about 10-14 days, can't remember, but I think two weeks was about right.

I got my orders at the completion of the training at the Combat Center and they were going to send me right back to the 26th

Engineers, E Company. I just spent my last 18 months in Vietnam with that unit before I got out in 1970. I hitched a ride to the personnel center at main post, got a hold of one of the personnel clerks and requested to be sent somewhere different. My primary MOS (Military Occupation Skill) was Combat Engineer (12F20) but my secondary MOS was Cavalry Scout (11D20). The clerk told me that they had some openings in the Cavalry; did I want to go there? He stated that they were in a place called Khe Sanh up north. I said, "Ya, that sounds good to me." Now this took a couple of days, so it gave me time to ask were Khe Sanh was. When I found out it was the same place were the Marines were back in 68, I started to have a couple of second thoughts.

George retired from the military after 22 years, 11 months, and 27 days, but who's counting, he says. The highest honor that a solider can achieve is to serve his country in the time of War. Two quotations that have stayed with me through all the years were read off a latrine wall in Vietnam in 1967. They are: "Life is like a crock of shit with the handles on the inside" and "Their is no such thing as gravity, the whole world sucks", authors unknown.

2/18-25/1971, (Can't remember the exact date), they put me on a 2 ½ ton truck(duce and ½) and drove me and others to a town called Hue. Put more supplies and people on, then they drove me to another town called Quang Tri. Same thing, people, supplies, and mail (then I realized that I was on what they called the milk run, stops everywhere). Now it's starting to get a little dark (I have been on this truck for about 8-10 hours and my butt was starting to like the rails on the truck). Well, this was the last stop. Next stop Khe Sanh! They drove us through all the bad areas without mishap. Of course the driver was going as fast as he could (no one was worried about getting hit, we were worried about falling out of the truck) and it was damn hard to stay in the truck.

Made it to Khe Sanh, met with the rear people and they told me that I would be with C Troop, 3rd Platoon, and they were out in their night defensive position for the night. I could go out with the chow truck. So I gathered all my gear and put it in the chow truck, a ¾ ton truck. It took us about 30-45 minutes to get to the defensive position which was not to far off the road.

I got all my stuff together and they introduced me to the Platoon Sergeant Thompson. He asked me what type of experience did I have in Viet Nam? I told him that I was Tank Commander (TC) of an Engineer tank and I would feel more comfortable in a tank, so he took me to C-39, a Sheridan tank (I did not remember the names of these guys until about 33 years later). He introduced me to the crew, TC was Steve Rockwell, driver was Ron Castor, gunner can't remember, and loader was ??. He was a what they call KC Scout (Kit Carson Scout), once a VC (Viet Cong) who turned sides. Something like the Indian scouts did during the Indian wars. I was the fifth man on the tank and the fifth man on a tank is what they call the "Rear Deck Gunner." What that means is I rode the rack on the outside of the tank.

Now as time goes on and as the events go on you will understand why I could not remember their names. It was dark. I have been in the Platoon for about an hour, been on the road since early that morning, around 0600 (6:00 AM) and it was around 2030 hours (8:30PM). The TC tells me to catch some sleep, that I would not be doing any guarding that night. Got my stuff together and laid down on the ground some where behind the tank to get some ZZzzzzz.

Well, about an hour or so later all hell broke lose. Mortar rounds were hitting inside the perimeter, RPG's (Rocket Propelled Grenades) were going off, people were shouting, guns starting to fire. I jumped to my feet and leaped onto the back of the tank. I was standing on the back deck holding on to the storage rack, waiting for the ground attack. Now the reason the 3rd Platoon was guarding this site was a helicopter refueling site and we had some Arvin's (South Vietnamese Soldiers) on the right flank and the rest of the perimeter was ACAV's of the 3rd Platoon.

Back to the story. As I said, rounds were going off. There was a chopper burning. I don't know if it got hit with a mortar or an RPG. I noticed in the middle of the logger position a gunner of one of the choppers was firing his M-60 machine gun and his chances of hitting friendlys was great. Now I don't remember this part well but I know they were hollering at the machine gunner to seize fire because he had friendlys in front of him and they did not want anybody to get shot by friendly fire. This is where it gets foggy. I think I ran out to the guy and told him to stop firing and to get into a bunker. If it was not me someone else did it. It just seems like I did.

Back to the tank. Now all this time the tanks were firing their machine guns and firing rifles. I did not have any ammo being a new guy so I yelled at the TC to give me some ammo. He turns around and hands me 1 magazine. I gave him a wild look and hollered "Is this all you have?" He told me that was all he could find. Well needless to say I wasn't going to waste my ammo just shooting since all I had was 1 magazine. I was going to save it for the human wave attack if it comes (now you have to remember this is where the Marines were getting overran in 1968). Thinking of a human wave attack was reasonable to me at the time. The shooting goes on for about 15-20 minutes more, then all of a sudden the front of the Sheridan lights up, the tank rocks back real hard giving me whiplash, and I was blinked from the flash. I was thinking that the tank got hit with an

RPG round, but when the smoke cleared, I realized the Sheridan had fired a flachett round (The round held 10,000 little darts, very effective for close combat). I didn't hear any command that they were going to fire and I didn't hear fire in the hole plus I was to busy looking in the rear for enemy dinks coming in through our perimeter. They caught me off guard. They fired a couple of more rounds after that, then a cease-fire was given.

George holding an RPG (Rocket Propelled Grenade)

It was found out later that some sappers came in through the ARVN side of the perimeter. I don't think we got any kills out of this for no one checked. Things kinds of went back to normal and everybody stayed up just a little longer before settling down. That was my first night with 3rd Platoon, C Troop 1/1 Cavalry. Kind of hard to forget that night.

2/28/1971, Howard Sidney Lamb, Gadsden, Al, Small Arms Fire, 4W/12

The next day we pulled out and went up in the mountain area. I really don't have any idea where we were at that time. Did not have a map or did any one show me where we were on a map, but I know we were in the mountains. Now these mountains are steep! Some places were over 1000 foot drop. The roads were only wide enough for one vehicle to go at a time. Some of the roads were so steep that we had to put the vehicles in reverse to come down. The steep areas were not too long, not more than 100 meters long, but scary.

As you know I am still the rear deck gunner, so my place is to sit behind the TC. I had a couple of flak jackets that I would use for a seat, trying to make it soft. If you know anything about a Sheridan, they turn on a dime. I know what you are thinking; well it did happen and they threw me off the tank. The tank made a hard left and I went right, right to the ground. When I looked up all I saw was dust going away from me before they noticed that I was missing. They stopped and backed up. I was glad they did, no complaints from me, and I just paid more attention and hung on.

We drove around for a week or so up there. Our presence kept Charlie away for I don't recall any encounters while we were up there.

Anthony John Newman, "Faces,"
Some of my memories live on in faces,
Never mind religion, politics, or races,
Fuckin' Steven, Fuckin' Mike,
You know who you be,
Hogie and Jungle George,
Arkie, Dave, an Timmy,
Al, Rich, and Frenchie,
Doc Moyer and J.C.
Harley, Eskimo, J.J., Watikie,
Erkle, Bro Reggie, an Bro Slim,
All fighting in a war,
Where to live is to win.

3/1/1971, We stopped for a maintenance break while still in the mountains. We were having problems starting our tank, some kink of charging problem so the driver was slaving it off and the next thing I know is everybody was running and shouting, "Get out, get out, she's going to blow!" I looked up and saw smoke coming from the tank and everybody was getting away from it. Now the reason everybody was getting away was that a Sheridan's main gun rounds are very flammable and a flash fire is expected (Note: each round has a fire proof cover but I don't think all the rounds had one). Yep, she burned to the ground. All that was left was a set of tracks with a big blob of metal in the middle.

That ended my career as a tanker in the Cavalry. I got with the platoon leader, Beaufort Hallman, and Platoon Sergeant Thompson and requested to be put on an ACAV (113 APC). Something a little safer, if there is such a thing. They took me to C-32, James Dean was the TC, and I became his left gunner. I don't remember who the other crewmen were as again I was the new guy. Now Sgt. Dean, his track was the lead track, which meant that he was the first track in the Platoon. If our Platoon was leading the Troop, then he was the first in the lead, kind of a prestigious position.

We moved off the hill and down to the road, QL-9, which is the main road that led to the Laos boarder. I believe that it was C Troops mission to keep this road open so that when the South Vietnamese Army comes back the road will be open for them. Now let me tell you the NVA (North Vietnamese Army, or the bad guys) had every intention of closing that road and wiping out the South Vietnamese Army and any Americans that got in the way. The last couple of miles of that road was very intense fighting from the Cavalry and the Infantry elements that were supporting this operation. In all 3rd Platoon made at least 13 trips up and down this road. That's the ones I counted (yes, we were counting, everybody makes a trip).

We rotated Platoons and I think B Troop went down a couple of times. I don't remember everything of each trip but just some of the events that happen while making those trips. This road later was known as Ambush Alley.

We moved down to lower ground were the hills where small compared to the ones up on that mountain. When we first got there, no one had any jackets or cold weather clothing and believe it or not, it was cold up there in Khe Sanh. I can remember all of us complaining about the cold weather at night. I guess it got down to 70 or in the 60's at night (now that is cold when you are used to the weather never going below 75). Well they ordered an emergency supply of field jackets and sleeping bags. Yes, sleeping bags for the troop and we were happy after that, and warm. During this whole operation we rarely came in contact with the other platoons. We operated independently of each other by being on each other's flank (that's left or right sides).

3rd Platoon moved down to our logger location (that's a defensive position). I am going to refer to this location a lot but I can't remember the name we gave it, or it's hill number. I remember it as the hill where the Air Force had a ground unit and they were in charge of operating a beacon for the B-52 bombers flying bombing missions to Laos and back

Every time a platoon left this hill another platoon took it's place until the Air Force people moved off. Now this defensive position was right at the beginning of QL-9 were the shit is hitting the fan, if you get my drift. One side of the hill we could observe 300-500 meters of QL-9 and on the side I was on about 500 meters of QL-9. The rest of the perimeter was elephant grass about 12-15 feet high. We were about 3 miles from the Laos boarder. We did a lot of scouting in that area with our vehicles and conducted some ground searches. Walking in the thick grass was difficult and you could be with in 10 foot of a track and not see it. We drove around in that stuff off and on and came across a couple of T-62's from the Soviet Union and a couple of destroyed Marine bulldozers from 1968. Made a couple of trips to the river if that's what you want to call it. In some places you could wade across. Our side was Viet Nam and the other Laos. We did our duty there; wrote what we thought of Viet Nam, pissed in the water, and I think one fellow swam across and wrote some choice names in the sand. We felt a lot better after that.

For about the next 30 days or so everything gets a little foggy. Time frame, mid March to mid April or about.

I am going to break this part of the story into two locations that I am familiar with. Reason is I don't remember in what order the events accrue in. One, the hill where the B-52 beacon was for the bombers, and two, QL-9, forward of the Air Force hill we were staying on, Ambush Alley. I think most of us that can't remember the 1SGT's name or the guy that shot at him.

Grant Coble

Here's how I remember the story. We had this PFC (E-3) that was Tank Commander on one of the Sheridans. He was an old timer (meaning he had over 6 months in country) and a bunch of new guys came in about a week before this, and a Sergeant was going to be the new TC. So one thing lead to another and this brings us to the point of the story.

An argument started between them both and the PFC Jap Slapped (meaning he knocked the crap out of him) the Sergeant. The Sergeant went and told the LT who promptly went over to talk to him and one thing led to another when the PFC told the LT to get off his tank before he shot him. There was a lot of shouting going on and by this time everyone in the perimeter knew the Sergeant was slapped and we were waiting to see what was going to happen next.

Anthony John Newman, "Top,"
Too many shammers, loafing in the rear,
I'm sending them to the field,
With re-supply and beer.

Nine men on a track,
A snipers delight,
Men crowded back to back,
Not ready to fight.

Is this kind of idiocy really us?
Or just one man's logic we can't trust?
We must push on, we must, we must!
Deros is coming, it's that or bust.

The LT and the PFC argued back and forth some more. Someone called the 1SGT who was back in the rear. Now one must remember that we had not received hot chow in about 6 weeks and this was the 1SGT's job to insure we did, which he rarely did. So, here comes the 1SGT's jeep. He jump's out, walks towards the tank yelling, "*^%$^ put that %#@ weapon down!" The PFC takes aim between the 1SGTs legs and fires. The 1SGT grabs his legs, turns around and gets back into his jeep and leaves. The PFC now gets scared, jumps into the driver's seat and shouts he is taking the tank to the Laos boarder and off he goes. He drives past me as the LT shouts to shoot him. We hesitated at first as you don't normally get a command to shoot one of your own. When the order sunk in we opened up with small arms fire which made little sense as one is not going to stop a tank with small arms and that's all we had. And besides the PFC secured the hatch. The LT called the other side of the perimeter and told them to destroy the tank as it approached if he would not stop.

Another Platoon put 2 tanks on the road loaded with heat rounds (High explosive anti tank). As the PFC approached he realized what lay in wait for him and stopped. He gave up, was flown to the rear, we recovered the tank, and all this happened before dark. Just another day in the Cavalry.

Now we stayed on and off this hill the whole time we were there until we left, and that is strange for the Cavalry for we never liked to stay in the same positions more than once. Doing so gave the VC a chance to get a bead on your location if you stayed too long. We were making "Thunder Runs" up and down the White Ball (dirt road) at night with ACAV's only. This was designed by some Officer some place to keep the NVA and VC from planting mines on the road. We hated this duty, but at least we rotated tracks while conducting this 2 or 3 mile run. "It Sucked!"

Well, one track did get hit with a RPG as it was turning around at the half way point. They left the area in a big hurry and raced back to our AO. They radioed back they had been hit so we were waiting for them. Here they came, slammed onto the brakes, and dropped the rear ramp. Out flew a million feathers in one big cloud. The RPG had hit the radio bracket where the sleeping bags had been stored. The crew had been stationed, or riding, on top, which is normal for an ACAV crew and no one was hurt.

As I mentioned, the Dink's checked us out and one night about O-Dark-Thirty where they found a breach in our defense and came in. The Ground Troops and Sappers (Little people who like to blow things up) were attacking and trying to blow things up inside our perimeter. There was some very intense fighting: Dink's running around, things blowing up, people shouting, small arms shooting, machine guns firing, tanks firing main guns, radio blaring. It just got a little confusing some times.

I remember telling the guys to shoot anyone that got near our tank and I think this was understood by all in the Platoon. You and Sappers on the ground at the same time is not too cool. Well, wouldn't one know it but JJ, or Junkie John (didn't know his real name for 33 years), was on the ground using his machete. A radio message warned all to be on the look out for him. I would say he was just a little excited. This little encounter lasted for about 30 to 60 minutes or somewhere in there. It was still dark, but now quiet. We stayed up until dawn to see what damage there was. We suffered no KIA's, but some wounded.

The Air Force guys had a bunker and a air conditioned GP tent, 16 foot by 32 foot, loaded with communications equipment. There was a Mars Station also and the Air Force guys called home each night. Everything in the tent was new: cots, equipment, mosquito netting, weapons, clothing, and anything else a soldier might need. This is what the Dink's were after. We arrived in their area just as they were getting out of the bunker at dawn. They had stayed in it all night. I think some of them thought the end of the world was upon them that night. They were not used to this type of environment (Hostile environment).

2 hours later their chopper picked them up and they left with out their supplies. It was like Christmas for us. We salvaged what we wanted, including ½ case of whiskey before the LT ran us back to our tracks.

I don't know much about this road (QL-9, Ambush Alley). I do know it crosses over into Laos. This isn't like roads we have back home. It's cut with bulldozers through the jungle. A clearing is cut about 10-15 feet back most of the time which gives us a little breather from the elephant grass. The road was very dangerous as about 2-3 NVA regiments were well dug in and waiting for someone to pass. We counted each trip we made. The last mile had a destroyed vehicle about every 20 or so feet including one helicopter.

We lost a lot of vehicles on this road and that is why we counted trips. The trip I most remember was with James Dean, my TC. I don't know why we were going down that road but we were in the lead. Each track had 5 crew members. The TC, driver, left and right gunner, and rear guard (between the gunners). Each track had a 50 cal and two M-60's with 2000 to 3000 rounds for the 50 and 15,000 to 20,000 for the M-60's. James sometimes carried another M-60 in the TC hatch to add to side fire power. Whitey, the middle man had a M-16 with about 150 to 200 20 round clips plus 2 or 3 cans of extra ammo.

We turned a corner and all hell broke loose. We were setting on top when the first Whoosh of many sent us inside. We began firing everything we had. A quick look at the TC and driver brought some humor to the moment as both looked like they were twisting and turning to avoid the onslaught. With the next Whoosh I looked up and watch one RPG coming straight at my head. I watched in awe as it closed in, ducked at the last moment, and Twang. The fin hit my helmet, knocking it off, wounding Whitey and the right gunner (these were light wounds a bandage would take care of). Whitey hits me on the shoulder and pointing to his smoking flak jacket, pierced ear, and cuts.

We made it through as did the other tracks. If they had knocked us out then the other tracks behind us would have been trapped and easier targets, but it didn't work this time. We completed our mission and made the return trip, however, this time we were more prepared and blazed our way through.

Another trip was to retrieve some Arty guys and destroy their equipment if time allowed. We loggered up in a defensive position waiting while the guys loaded up when some NVA artillery opened up on us. We hit the dirt or found fox holes to crawl into. One round hit the ammo dump setting off more explosions and fires. We remounted and left the area. One of our tracks got hit. We stopped to pick them up and in the confusion another track ran into the back of us, disabling it. Taking on their crew now gave us 10 men on a 4 man track. People were crammed in every which way.

This was an every day thing on QL-9. Body counts were never taken but according to the chopper pilots, many lay in the piles along the road (not ours).

It was seldom we made a night march but we did this one time (Dangerous to ones health). As we began to move out, a battery of

155 took on a fire mission. They were located alongside the road and to reload they had to lower the barrels. Therefore, we had to move only when the barrel was raised to fire and when they did, the concussion lifted the ACAV off the road. We did finally clear the area and not to soon, for our hearing was being impaired (You say something? What?).

We were now down to a few tracks per Platoon. We had 1 tank, 2 APC's, and a Mortar Track left running. Platoon Sergeant Beafort Hallman was now on our track and his 3rd track as the other 2 were disabled. James Dean was now a driver as no one else would drive. We also had Sniper Everett Lawrence along which gave us 6 men on one track; too many. Again we were going down QL-9, but this time it was the whole Platoon plus some tanks (M-48's) from the 1-77 Armor and a Duster (M-48 chassie mounted with 2 40MM cannons). There must have been 15-20 vehicles in this convoy and for the first time we were last, eating everybody's dust as we went.

The next sequence of events went something like this. I was setting on top of the loaders hatch (that's where we all sat so as not to get our legs shot off from an RPG or mine) when "Bang!" I'm rising in the air and falling back to the track. The smell of gun powder is strong. A mine! The driver's chin has been slammed into the drivers hatch. We scream for him to "Stop, stop," but he can't as the track and some choice other parts have been blown off and we travel another 10 to 15 feet before stopping. We quickly dismount for fear the track will blow up as the mine went off under the fuel tank.

Realizing the track may not blow, the TC and I crawl back into the track. While the TC grabs the radio and calls C-36 to inform him we hit a mine, I grab a M-60 and a can of ammo and dismount again. A tank shows up and not 30 feet from us hits another mine. He starts firing his main gun in a 360 degree pattern. A duster shows up next and also begins the same pattern. Now we begin to worry as we think the mines were command detonated and the NVA are right here. We are now waiting for the ground attack and be wiped out.

The LT and I were standing behind the track, he with radio and me with the M-60. I was about to spray the elephant grass, but yelled out as I did not know where the rest of the crew was. A loud reply kept me from spraying the elephant grass as the rest of the crew was hiding there. They came out. Dean, the driver, had a bad gash on his chin. I think another guy was also hurt. The LT called in a dust off as the rest of 3rd Platoon showed up. Two of us stayed with the track until it was picked up. Dean did not come back and I became C-32's new Track Commander.

We had been eating 20 year old C-Rats, like from WW-11. Some of the guys got sick eating them and we figured it was the spaghetti or the beef and guts, so no one would eat them. Now the pound cake and peaches, everyone liked, and was like gold. Well, the time came when we had to turn in all the C-Rats, some 200-300 cases. A "Big" fire was started and that was the last of that food source.

The incident that I'm about to cover is not pretty, a black eye to the Cav. A Sister Troop refused to go and retrieve a secured radio left by them. They had relieved us on QL-9 and had received casualties as we had. By military standards this is mutiny. The word came down from the Squadron Commander to Captain Nuccitelli to send a Platoon out and relieve that troop. So here goes 3 Platoon again to QL-9. We arrived about 0600 or 0700 and what do we find, a big fire in the middle of the logger with those on guard around it, a "Big NO NO." Some one should have been on guard on each track and no one was. They offered us hot coffee or chocolate and told us why they refused but over the years I've forgotten the reason.

Later we heard the officers and NCO's had all been replaced in the unit.

Another situation arrived during our stay on or near QL-9. A Cobra chopper went down and we were sent to guard it. When we arrived not a soul was around. The rockets were either on the ground or half hanging from the rocket tubes so we stayed clear. When the recovery team arrived, they stripped the chopper of all its vital gear and informed us that was all they were taking. We were informed we would destroy the chopper, but first we stripped the chopper of the goodies we wanted. The soft, high back seats went to C-32, which now gave us the "Real" look of a gypsy wagon.

The word came down that the NVA had sent 4 T-39 tanks to finish us off. Now this worried us as we had not fought against tanks before. The Sheridans were lined up in a good defensive position and

Grant Coble

we were issued LULL's, 2 each, and placed in fox holes to ambush the tanks as they neared. We would race back to the ACAVS and man our 50's and finish off any tank not knocked out by the LULL's. The Air Force was given the job of trying to knock out the tanks by air before they got to us. Well, they did, and we were thrilled!

Orders came down for us to return to Khe Sanh's air strip for some rest and guard the air strip. We parked on the air strip and quickly realized this was a prime target for NVA artillery 3 times a day, 6 AM, 12PM, and 4PM, chow time. The bunkers near by were fully filled with GI's each time and getting into one was sometimes difficult. You could hear them go off, 4 seconds, and "Bang!"

On the 3rd day we took a direct hit on one of the tracks and lost 2 crew members. One of their fellow crew members ran to the ACAV as it began to burn to try and get the 2 guys out to no avail. We received a new CO that day, Captain Steven May, and moved out, leaving the burning track and fellow troopers inside.

3/1971 to 7/1971, Stephen May, Captain, Troop Commander

Anthony John Newman, "Views,"
Spit at, cussed at, flipped off and more,
The Vietnam Veteran, this decade's whore.
Shamed by factors out of control,
The Vietnam Veteran, now a friendless sole.
Blamed by the multitudes for all kinds of sin,
The Vietnam Veteran, wasn't allowed to win.
He served this country with honor and pride,
The Vietnam Veteran may as well have died.
The soldier is suffering memories untold,
The Vietnam Veteran, trying to keep hold.
Ignored and abused, by family and friend,
The Vietnam Veteran is rising again.
With tempered strength learned in the bush,
The Vietnam Veteran is starting to push.
Dumping the labels, growing strong fast,
The Vietnam Veteran will surely win.
Where are the citizens that sentenced us there,

The Vietnam Veteran knows they don't care.
Who will fight the next righteous war,
The Vietnam Veterans asks no more, no more.

As we passed the burning track we remembered this game was for keeps. Our next mission was the Rock Pile, some 10 clicks, or 6 miles away.

The Rock Pile was a large formation with lots of space for us to set up and conduct maintenance on weapons and tracks. On an outcrop near by we saw some Apes, or monkeys with tails as long as their bodies. Someone asked permission to test fire their 50 and was given the OK. He opened up on the monkeys, scattering them. Others seeing this also open up. The CO realizing what was happening ordered a seize fire, much to the scattering monkeys delight. This may seem heartless, but we had just lost 2 of our Brothers and tension was high.

From the Rock Pile we went to Dong Ha, on to QL-1, to Quang Tri, Hue, and finally to Phu Bai, Camp Eagle, a 101st Airborne base camp. Here we stood down for re-supply. Our Platoon arrived with about 10 to 15 personnel from our full complement of 40 per Platoon. We had 2 113's, one Sheridan, and one mortar track.

One of the first things we noticed upon arrival was the 101st swimming pool. The LT received permission for us to use the pool and with out too much waste of time, we were in. One must remember we hadn't showered or bathed in some 60 days and, while none of us had noticed, others did. As the water in the pool began to turn a dark brown the pool manager chased us out. I understand some 2 weeks later they were still trying to clean the water.

Anthony John Newman, "Hurrah,"
Young men and boys sent to fight,
In countries far away,
Believing that their cause is right,
An enemy to slay.

Knowing on returning home,

Grant Coble

They'll receive a big hooray,
Many years past the war,
Still waiting for that day.

3/6/1971, Carl Wronko, During a rocket attack at Khe Son, Stephen Brugdorfer, Horace Bruton, and Tomas Valerio jumped into the same fox hole. Once the rocket attack subsided, they jumped from the fox hole only to be hit by one last rocket that landed next to them. Brugdorfer and Bruton died out right and Valerio was seriously wounded and taken to the Squadron Aid Station only yards away. Tom was dusted off to the Hospital ship, Repose, of which he died of his wounds the next day **(see 3/7/1971)**

3/6/1971, Stephen Walter Brugdorfer, Vane, PA, Ground Casualty, 4W/27

3/6/1971, Horace Lee Burton, Texarkana, AR, Ground Casualty, 4W/27

3/7/1971, I first met Thomas Valerio at Fort Knox, Ky. In February 1970. As a young Butter Bar or 2nd Lt., being the lowest ranking officer in the Brigade, I was assigned to various and miscellaneous Battalion and Brigade duties as the Duty Officer. A young shake and bake Sgt. was assigned to one of the Troops in the Brigade and being the lowest ranking Sgt. in the Brigade, he soon found himself being the Sgt. of the Guard, Brigade NCOIC, Brigade Weapons Control NCO. The Sergeant was Thomas Valerio who haled from Staten Island, Ny.

I was from New Jersey and we had a lot in common. Being assigned together quite often we became good friends. Many was the night that he and I sat up together, telling stories of home, our girl friends, our Mom's cooking, and our plans for when we got out of the Army. We extended our friendship outside of our Army duties, going together to Louisville to chase the young ladies together.

In the middle of April 1970, my assignment was changed from the Training Brigade to the Commanding General's staff and I lost touch with Tom. I was subsequently given orders to Vietnam where I joined C Troop. During this time, Tom also was given orders to Vietnam and was assigned to the 11th Armored Cav. In December 1970 our paths crossed again. Tom had gotten in country in May

1970; and, those with less than 9 months in country were assigned to other units in Vietnam. Tom was sent to C Troop and arrived in December 1970, with about 5 months left in country.

By this time, I was the XO of C Troop and stationed in our rear area. When Tom walked into the Troop Headquarters it was a pleasant surprise and we spent a good part of the day talking and getting caught up on our lives. He had bought and paid for a brand new Chevy convertible that he was going to pick up upon his DEROS and separation from the Army.

Since he still had 5 months left in country and was newly assigned to the unit, I should have sent Tom out to the field to join the Troop as a Track Commander. We had a lot of other Sergeants out in the field with more time in country, and more service with C Troop, who in the sequence of things deserved to get out of the field before Tom. I knew what I should do, but I couldn't do it. I assigned Tom to the Troop Armory as an Assistant Armor. In due course, the Troop along with the Squadron was tasked to be part of the Lam Son operation in Khe Son, thus, the invasion of Laos by the Arvin.

C Troops rear was in time moved up to Khe Son. I was still in the process of going back and forth between Chu Lai and Khe Son, coordinating the movement of our unit's assets up to Khe Son. The last time I saw Tom, it was at Khe Son where the Troop's Armory was located, and he had just gotten a Dear John Letter from his girlfriend. He was down about it as you can imagine, but he was picking himself up by thinking of his new car.

While in Chu Lai I heard that the area where C Troop's rear was at Khe Son had been hit by NVA Artillery or Rockets and that some of our personnel had been badly wounded. When I got back up there I found out Tom was one of those who had been badly wounded on March 7, 1971. It seems that he and two others from the Troop had jumped into a slit trench to take cover from the incoming rounds. When the incoming rounds stopped, Tom and the other 2 got out of the trench, just as one last rocket came in. I was told that Tom had lost both his legs at the crotch area but that he was still alive when taken to the Squadron Aid Station, which was just a few yards away form where he was wounded. I went to the Aid Station to find out what I could and was told that he had been immediately evacuated out to the Navy Hospital Ship Repose and that they knew nothing else.

Later, I stopped while in Chu Lai at Division personnel to see if they could tell me anything about Tom, but they could not. When I got home, I thought of trying to find Tom at his home in NY. But, for whatever reason, I could not do this. Many years later, when visiting the Wall in Washington, DC for the first time, I looked up Tom's name. I found it - Panel 4W, Line 32. I think I knew it all the time but could not face it. Over the years since, I have often wondered what would have happened if I had assigned Tom to a Platoon rather than to the Troop Armory. I will never know. I have since looked to see if anyone else from the Troop died on the same day as Tom in an attempt to find the others who were wounded when he was, but they must have survived their wounds, or perhaps they succumbed to them on a different date than he did.

3/7/1971, Tomas Valerio, New York, NY, Rocket Blast, 4W/32

3/15/1971, Philip Robert Jamrock, Burnham, IL, RPG, 4W/49

3/21/1971, Alan Eunice Davis, Tulace, California, Explosive Device, 4W/63

3/21/1971, Ron Dougherty, In 1984, as I started going to the Wall and started the personal healing process, there were several names I remembered from day one. Joe Crenshaw, Tom Lafferty, and Phillip Jamrock were names that instantly came to me.

However, there was one guy I remembered but could not remember his name. The details of his death stuck with me; it could have been me as easily as it had been him. His death has always bothered me for that reason. Why could I remember the details of his death so very well, but could not remember his name?

On the day of his death, several of us were in the rear near Lang Vei. We had been sent there the day before on tracks that needed repaired.

Claudius, Dave Cooper, and myself were going to test fire our M-60' that we had spent the morning repairing. We walked across the dirt road where a test firing range had been developed. As we waited our turn, we shared stories regarding home and our dreams for the future. Claudius also shared photographs he had of his sisters.

Evidently, it became our turn to test fire. We walked up to the firing line and started shooting our M-60's in a variety of firing positions. As I fired mine for awhile, it jammed (around got stuck and would not fire). Claudius, who was more experienced, told me to stand the weapon with its butt on the ground; then kicked the bolt and it should un-jam. Never thinking about the consequences, I did exactly as he told me. And he was right. The shell ejected and it was ready for more firing. I continued to test fire for a few more minutes before quitting.

After I stopped firing, I watched for a little while longer and talked with Claudius. I told him I was going to go put my weapon away and would meet them at the track.

I had taken no more than 10 steps when I heard a weapon fire. For some reason, it sounded different than normal. An automatic OMG (Oh My God) type moment. Before I could take another step, I looked at a guy who was walking toward the test firing range. His face showed the horror. I turned around to see what had happen an saw Claudius lying on the ground in a pool of blood.

After Claudius was dusted off, I talked to Cooper who was still with him at the time of the accident. Cooper's weapon had jammed just like mine had. Instead of Cooper doing what I had done to un-jam mine, Claudius had done it for him. Unfortunately, when the shell came un-lodged, it fired instead of ejection. The shell hit Claudius in the forehead and exited the rear of his skull. Most likely killing him instantly.

In 2000 shortly after I met Carl Wronko online, I quizzed him about the incident. He kind of remembered the incident but couldn't remember a name. With his guidance, I started researching various web sites dealing with the KIA's from the Vietnam War. Finally in February of 2001, I was able to narrow it to Claudius Small; Which turned out to be the right name. Finally locating the name turned into a healing process for me.

In November of 2001 on my first trip to the Wall after finding Claudius' name, I was able to say "Hi" to him. Part of that trip was my apology to him for not remembering the name even though I had

Grant Coble

never forgotten him. Now as I visit the Wall, I can pay the respect to him that I have paid to the others since 1984.

3/21/1971, Claudius Augustus Small, San Juan, PR, Accident, 4W/64

3/22/71, Larry Dewayne Leamon, Harrison, TN, Explosive Device, 4W/67

3/23/1971, Manasseh Brock Warren, Washington, DC, Rocket, 4W/72

3/26/1971, Martin Reinholdt Huart Jr, Addison, IL, Accident, 4W/80

3/26/1971, Otto Tom Weben, Fort Lauderdale, FL, Ground Casualty, 4W/82

3/27/1971, Sheldon John Burnett, Pelham, NH, Helicopter Crash (MIA), 4W/31

1971, LTC Gene L. Breeding, Squadron Commander

3/30/1971, Terry Lee Bosworth, Whitmore, CA, Explosive Device, 4W/94

Mid April, May 71, George V. Robbins, Still at Camp Eagle in Phu Bai, we got a bunch of new guys (FNG's), new equipment, some old which brought us up to about 75% to 80% with about 80% in new guys. Memorial services were held for our fallen brothers which was a sobering moment. 22 pairs of boots and helmets were lined up on the stage, symbols of each fallen brother. This may not have represented only Charlie Troop's KIA. Rumors began to circulate that we were going to A Shaw Valley. We voiced our opinions to the CO that back to back rough missions, less than good equipment, and 80% new guys was not a good idea not to mention the terrain was not suited for armored tracks.

Whether this was a true rumor or not, we didn't go, but headed for our new home base of Camp Faulkner, just outside of Da Nang.

We pulled into the base camp in our traditional smoke bomb parade, letting everyone know the Cavalry was back in town. The first person I saw was the PFC that took a shot at the 1st Sergeant. He now was a supply clerk. Wouldn't you know it! Many of the guys wounded in Khe San had rear jobs. James Dean was the "Water Boy." We pulled our first mission after 3 days at camp.

Dragoons

I hitched a ride back to Chu Lai to visit some old engineer friends. Captain May and I had an agreement that if I could persuade any of them to transfer to our unit 3rd Platoon would get them. After some convincing, Billy Powel and David Spears agreed. We had served together on my previous tour in the Engineers. Billy was placed on a Sheridan and David to my track. Dave and I were very close and when you saw one of us you saw both of us.

We went back to Khe Sanh and upon arrival a request was made for someone to take over last track position. I did not want the lead position anymore so I volunteered. The nice part about this position you had one mechanic and one medic on your track. The down side was the dust, and when in base camp, only you and the driver worked on your track. While in column you always knew who was in front of you and who was behind you. This made it easy when pulling into a night defense position.

5-10/1971, Around dusk we pulled into our nightly defense position. We knew the area was heavily mined with anti-personnel mines as some of the tracks had hit them.. These will not disable a track but will maim or kill a person that steps on or trips one. We put out our RPG screens first. These chain link fences will stop an RPG from hitting your track, thus reducing the chances of one of us from getting hurt. I had 3 hits alone and many of the other tracks had as many as I. We began to set our trip flares and clamor mines next. There was an old railroad track about 20 foot in front of us with a culvert under it. This was a good place to cover so Siebers and I began placing our stuff around this. "Crunch!" I froze, asked Dave if he'd stepped on some dry grass, and "No" was the reply. I bent down to check and sure enough, 3 prongs were stuck into my boot.

Anthony John Newman, "RPG,"
Sundial form violates anything born,
Ruptured an pitted, burns metal with scorn.

Flesh and bone, cast askew,
Blood of friends, creates a hellish hue.

Killing and maiming, without regard,
That pyrotechnic assassin does not find it hard.

Grant Coble

I stood there for the longest 5 minutes of my life trying to figure out what I was going to do. We notified C-36 that mines were in the area and to let the others know. Dave went for a can of 45 caliber ammo. He was going to cut off my boot and replace my weight with the can. Dave had a fit when I told him I was going to walk away from the mine with out the ammo can on it. I removed my weight from the mine and headed back to the track. If it had not gone off by that time it most likely was a dud. I went back and marked the mine, did not finish setting the rest or our stuff, and spent the next 2 hours getting my color back. The next day we blew the mine which left a nice big hole in the ground.

During this operation we found a large bunker complex on a hill and called for some engineers to blow it. While waiting 2 Sheridans and 1 ACAV from 17th CAV approached. They had become separated from their unit and with some directions were off again. They went into a valley, following the hill when ambushed by VC. 3rd PLT got the word and off we went again. When we cleared the bottom of the hill we went hot, or all guns blazing. This lasted for some 15 minutes. When all the shooting was done, I think the VC had won this battle. One Sheridan and crew was destroyed. The other Sheridan had some damage as well as the ACAV with wounded. We dusted off the KIA and WIA and took the others with us. We did not go into the woods to see if we had killed any of the attackers. We figured it was at least a Platoon if not larger and were most likely waiting for us as this was the direction we were heading.

Another mission was to check out some bunkers. We either flew in or walked in, I remember not, but there was a lot of us and that meant there were few on the tracks. I don't remember where the tracks were even located. At one point we split into two groups of about 5 or 6 men. We started to check out each bunker. We all were in the open. An AK-47 opened up on us and I hit the dirt so fast my steel pot flew off, leaving my squad members to believe I was dead. The bullets zinged pass my head so close I could feel them. I grabbed my steel pot and scrambled with the others to a position where we returned fire. Just before the VC opened up, the Squadron Commander and SST Bryson came to our location and witnessed the whole thing. I was put in for an medal for my actions during this, which I found out months later during a medal passing out ceremony.

During each operation a platoon will search out several locations each day for a night logger, or defensive position. It was 3rd Platoons job this day and with each location a foot recon is required. In one we found a empty village and checked it out. Now generally we do not follow foot paths because of booby traps and mines but this evening we did as it was getting late.

I was lead and followed the path. Something tugged at my foot and would not let go. Looking down, I saw to my horror a line caught on my dog tag laced to my shoe laces. I froze! The Kit Carson Scout was behind me and I relayed what happened. He backed up, told my good friend David Siebers what was happening. Nothing happened so I bent down and with very shaky hands untied the fishing line from the dog tags, quickly backed up and down the hill. My nerves were shot. The KC went back up the hill, followed the trip wire and found the grenade still in its packing container, all rusty. This is why the pin did not pull free. We removed the grenade, went to a well, and exploded the device. Yes, it was still functional. From this point on I kept my dog tags tucked under my shoe laces.

On another mission we spent most of our time in flooded rice paddies. The water must have been 2 foot deep and as not all the ACAVs were water tight, they were wet inside also. At night we would find a higher location. On one such night I walked up to one of the Sheridans only to find a large bomb under the tank. We vacated the hill at dark and sent a team back up to explode the bomb before we relocated again on the hill. It did not explode under the Sheridan because the tank cut the wires to the firing device. Had it not, I think the tracks on both sides would have also been hurt badly. It was a big one and left a big hole.

On this same mission one of the ACAVs got stuck and we spent the better part of the day and night trying to get it out to no avail, so we loggered up about 2 hundred yards from it. We spent the rest of the night in deep water, using 50 caliber cans to help keep our cots up out of the water. Each track carried a cot for each crew member. The next morning at day break we noticed the back door to

Grant Coble

the ACAV was open. We had stripped the track of all its vital items and secured the back door before deserting it that night. The LT let C-6 know what had transpired and that the area around the track and the track itself was most likely booby trapped. After some hours the word came down to destroy the track. The best Sheridan crew was mustered to the job. One heat round through the back door and "Blam," one huge explosion followed by a second. The track was totally destroyed. We called that gunner "Dead Eye" after that.

5/12/1971, Edelmiro Leonel Garcia Sr, Mercedes, TX, Explosive Device, 3W/33

6/21/1971, is a day I will never forget. It was 3rd Platoons time for a complete overhaul of vehicles. The tracks are stripped of all munitions and weapons which are secured in the arms room. Every Platoon goes through this every 3 months, 4 days of maintenance and 3 days of stand down. This was our last day and the club next door was well stocked. You close the club, go home, and fall asleep, fully dressed, just in case.

Well, in the early hours of morning, maybe even midnight, we heard the first loud "Boom!" Then a second. We all sat up and stared at each other. Someone yelled "Incoming" and we all made a wild dash for the door. The next round landed on the hutch next door, "Bang" as we cleared ours, and the next on ours. They had us zeroed in.

Some guys hit the dirt just outside of the hutches while others scattered. I figured that the best place was where one round had already landed. This proved wrong by the sheer numbers of motor rounds. 3 of us worked our way to the locked tracks and stood beside one wondering what to do next when 2 other guys showed up and slid under the ACAV. Not a good idea for if a round hits in front or rear, the effects will be funneled. The rounds were getting closer. They say you get a funny feeling seconds before a round is about to hit you, and we did. Seconds later a round landed in front of the ACAV. I felt like a sledge hammer hit me in the back of the head and I had a loud ringing in my ears.

I could not hear or see well and survival instincts were taking over. I took off running, losing track of the others. "Bang!" Another round landed near me, knocking me to my knees. I got up again and ran for some hutches near by. Ducking between them I was knocked to the ground. Stunned, I began feeling to see if my arms and feet still worked. Getting up I quickly realized why I'd been decked. A communications wire was stretched between the hutches and it clothes-lined me. I began to work my way towards the Medic station, which was next to the NCO club, a well known drinking hole. A soldier was coming out of a bunker as I passed and exclaimed, "Oh my God"(Now that's scary when you can't see yourself and trying to hold it together). I was covered in blood.

I made it to the aid station but no one was there. I hollered out and in the middle of the floor a door opened. They had their own bunker in the middle of the room. I told them I didn't think I was that bad but our area was hit hard and others might need their help more than I. Off they went, leaving me by myself.

The pool of blood was getting bigger when they began bring in wounded troopers. I think I must have been getting pale by this time and they began to check me over. One fellow took my dog tag and called me in KIA. Now this did not go down well and I protested loudly. I had some shrapnel in the back and buttock and a surface wound on the right side of my head above the ear. The trooper that jumped under the ACAV was wounded the worse. They dusted him off that night and we never saw him again. Of the 10 wounded, 2 were dusted off and the rest went out with the Platoon the next day. I went out the day after on a re-supply chopper.

Another incident involved the Squadron Commander. We were loggered up on the semi-hardtop to avoid mines as one of the lead tracks had hit one. The CO was working his way to the front to see what was happening and the Squadron Commander's track was with us for some unknown reason. Well, he didn't listen to the CO, and began to work his way up front when he hit a big mine, blowing the track some 25 foot into the air. It landed upside down. We ran to the track to see how many survived and helped. By this time the CO was there also and was asking the Squadron Commander how many men he had on board. He was incoherent, not even knowing his own name or how many men he had on board. Other than knocked silly, he was not hurt, or as we called it, punch drunk. We wanted to know how many men as we did not know and wanted to be sure all got out.

Grant Coble

Everything was piled up behind the driver's area and we could not tell if he got out. He stated 5 and we dusted them all off. The CO got the recovery track on location, picked up the track and the driver fell out, dead, as was the TC.

7/1971 to 4/1972, Robert Hains, Captain, Troop Commander

7/8/1971, Marion Tracy Griffin, Charlotte, NC, Explosive Device, 3W/104

7/9/1971 David Pitmon, When I was assigned to C Troop, I worked the Demo Track. After the injury at Pineapple Forest, I was reassigned to the Maintenance Section. This new Sergeant First Class came in and took over the section. If he didn't like you, then you were screwed. He jerked a lot of guy's around. I had less than 30 day's left in country when the unit was sent to the Arizona Territory. SFC Butthead ordered me to the field. I told him that was not right because of all the new guys that hadn't even been to the field. And still he ordered me out! I told that S.O.B. that if I was wounded I had better never see him again.

David "Cowboy" Pitmon

Dragoons

Four hour's after getting to the unit I was wounded by a mine that blew up under the Sheridan I was working on hit. I was sent back to the States and then to Germany.

God And The Soldier, Author Unknown, Donated By David Pitmon

All men adore
In times of trouble
And then no more
For when trouble
Is over and all
Things righted
God is forgotten
And the old
Soldier slighted

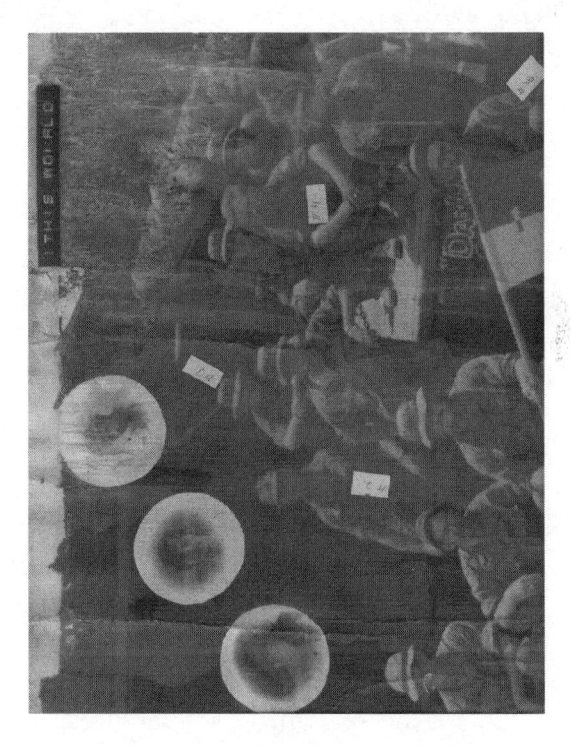

Maintenance Section 1. Bill McNabb 2. Benjamin 3. Sellers 4. John Ellis 5. Louis Shmidt 6. Cook

Grant Coble

I was sent to pick up some new guys. Entering the building, guess who I saw. "Yup!" Well, I did what I said I'd do and kicked his back side good. Every time I saw him I repeated the process and would still if I saw him.

Louie Schmidt standing in a new bunker with his shovel. C Troop out side of Dong Ha, South Vietnam.

George V Robbins, This little incident is in reference to my driver, Bobby Harrell. Now, as far as I'm concerned he was the best driver in the 1/1. It takes quite a bit of skill to drive a M-113 in the same tracks and they will only be a difference of ½ inch on the total width. This technique is known as tracking and he was good at it.

Back to the story. We have been into the operation about 2 weeks and were located in an area that was well fortified with enemy bunkers. The terrain was rough and the situation was tight, meaning we expected to get hit (attacked) at any time. We been at it for about an hour when the driver tells me on the intercom that he has to go. I ask, Go where?" He states that he has to take a dump. I explain to him that we can't stop here as we are in the middle of an operation and if he could hold it till we come to a break in the operation. He says Roger.

A couple of hours later he tells me that he can't wait any longer, he has to go! I get on the radio and give C-36 a call and inform him

Dragoons

we have to stop, my driver has to make a nature call. C-36 replies, "What the hell is a natures call?" I call back and inform him my driver has to take a dump and can't wait any longer and I have to stop. C-36 gives the order to stop. We are on the edge for this is a very dangerous area. Bobby jumps out, takes care of business, I get a few cat calls on the radio from the other TC's referencing why we stopped, and after the mission is completed, a little embarrassed driver climbs back into the track to continue the operation.

During one operation at night in our defensive Wagon Wheel position, set up as pioneers did, we had an unwelcome visitor. We had placed trip flares, clamors, and ground sensors out as well as RPG screens. The left M-60's were dismounted and placed on the ground for better ground cover. The grass in front of us was about 12-18 inches high. We were on 50% guard, or 2 men up per track. You have to remember, pulling guard during the wee hours of night can be very hard and falling asleep can be a problem. We sat back to back to eliminate this problem.

Well, a red flare went off. I must have been drowsy for at first I thought this strange but quickly realized we were under attack. Rockets were slamming into our encampment. The 50's opened up first followed by the M-60's. A wall of steel surrounded us, fanning out and saturating the surrounding area, a very impressive site for every 5th round is a tracer. After about 15 to 20 minutes all quieted down. No one was hurt nor any track hit. The next morning one VC was found dead.

On another mission we were working an area heavily defended with bunkers. We came on line and approached a wood line. I was at the far left of the LT and he was about 2 or 3 tracks from one of the Sheridans. A VC jumped from one of the bunkers and the LT opened up with his 45. The VC shot an RPG at the Sheridan, just missing the TC's head. The Tank went into hard reverse and took off. Everyone else opened up on the VC who quickly jumped back into the bunker. The Sheridan was still in hard reverse when the LT ordered them back on line. Another Sheridan was about ready to put a heat round into the bunker when 2 VC jumped up and ran. "BOOM!" That was the end of the bunker and the VC. No one was hurt.

One operation know as the "Round Up" took place in the Arizona Territory. 3rd Platoon was a blocking force while 1st and 2nd would rout out and drive the VC to us. We got a call that a Platoon size force was being pushed and trying to get away. We moved to a location after receiving the information, figuring this would be a good location for the ambush. We could hear small arms fire, a M-60, and a 50 once in a while open up. Now the radio is really busy with calls that they really have got them on the run. The Platoon that is chasing them knows we are ready so they begin to fall back as not to get shot themselves. We are now in the perfect position to give them hell when they enter the open. You can hear the noise in the trees and bushes of running bodies. There is no way anyone can escape this ambush.

The noise gets louder and we can hear people shouting from the other Platoon! All of a sudden a herd of pigs scramble from the bush, we open fire knowing that the VC are right behind pushing the pigs out. After a few minutes we seized fire and inform the other platoon we see only pigs. Some choice words and they know for a fact they were pushing VC. The Platoon clears the bushes. Only pigs this day. It took a long time for the other Platoon to live down this embarrassing moment and was there after know as the "VC Pig Attack."

1971, LTC Richard E. Lorix, Squadron Commander

11/20/1971, Joe L Love Jr, Wharton, TX, Explosive Device, 11W/126

Scott "Tex" Gideon, "I Did My Part,"

I went to war
I did my part
And lost my heart
God was with me
From the start
I went to war
I did my part
Rest in Peace

Dragoons

1972

2/1/1972, David Hill, This was to be our last mission out. I drove a Sheridan tank that had its hull twisted from hitting a landmine, but that wasn't unusual for the aluminum hulled Sheridan M-155.

Sheridans passing through a village in South Vietnam, battle laden and ready for action. Being the road was blacktop, was most likely French Highway 1.

    These light armor tanks were built for the Marines to be airdrop-able. In theory I suppose the concept was a good one, but they didn't seem to be able to take the punishment dished out by 19-year-old GI's, let alone Victor Charlie's bag of tricks.

    With the hull twisted as it was, we had to frequently change the idler wheel (the large cogged wheel in the front of the tank) due to the track running askew and wearing it down prematurely. The track was also made of aluminum links with rubber pads, as were the link pins, which would easily bend out of shape. It was impossible to remove a pin to loosen the track to allow us to remove the idler, so the field method we used was to pack the leading edge of the track with a shape-charge of C-4 and blow-it, drive off the old track onto a new one, hook it together and off we'd go.

I drove point. Sheridans typically ran point with a Beehive round in the tube. The plus side of this position was that I almost never got stuck in the churned-up muck from the other vehicles in line. The downside was, if there was a landmine to be hit………, well you get the idea.

David Hill sitting in the left gunners seat on a ACAV. This is the typical location gunners sat during missions out in the bush. The jeep seats came to the cavalry by what ever means necessary, including midnight re-supply.

Our normal missions were a rotation of 21 days in the field and 7 days of stand-down. This was the time when we would repair our vehicles and scrub the mud and sand out of them, and relax a few days before heading out again. This trip out was going to be 47 days straight, no showers, no major repairs, no PX, no comfortable cots.

We left Camp Faulkner, Danang and headed south past Marble Mountain with the artillery base perched on top, through the little vill, then turned west, We traveled familiar ground, but I couldn't tell you where we were on a map. I only heard in my headset, "Hill, turn right, Hill, head for that notch in the mountain ahead, Hill, SLOW DOWN!" I had gotten pretty comfortable with the performance of the tank, and would run it to the max, about 60 MPH on the hardball. With the hull being twisted, it would constantly pull to the right. All I had to do was jerk on the steering left every two seconds or so at that speed to keep her running straight.

One day, we fired the main gun, sort of as practice, at a large rock outcropping on a hillside. After a few HE rounds at the rock, our LT wanted to go up and look at what damage we had done. We had about 6 guys on 'patrol' up this hill to recon the rock. Surprisingly, it didn't show any signs of being hit. On the hike back down the hill, one guy found a paper bag of sorts lying on the ground. And, of course, he had to kick it to see if it would go off, I guess. It was a bag of what seemed to be CS gas. We di-di'ed down the mountain out of the smell and burning and just in case Chuck was nearby.

The Americal insignia, or patch worn by Americal Soldiers, painted on a large boulder near LZ Ross.

Once while we were running across a rice paddy, we came up on a stream with terraced banks, some mamma-sans were washing cloths or something down at the stream. My TC, Sgt. Cunningham, walked down the three terraces to the stream and guided me on to each level until I reached the water's edge. I could see that the tracks wouldn't span the banks to climb the other side. He insisted that I try to ford it. About 2/3 of the way across, the front of the tank dropped down, the driver's compartment flooded and the gun tube speared the opposite bank about 3 or 4 feet deep. Now I can't go forward, the tube was wedged in, I couldn't reverse up the terraces, I only had abut 2 foot of traction on the bank's edge. It took 3 APC's and the other Sheridan all connected with tow cables to hoist me out of the creek. Our loader had the bright idea to turn on the tube evacuator fan to clear the gun tube of mud, and he shot a clump of mud about 20 feet downrange.

About 45 days into the mission, we setup our NDP at the bend of a river. A few days before we were operating directly on the other side of the river. F Troop 2/1 Cav moved in on the side of the river we had just left. They had a UPI film crew onboard, recording "The Last Ground Combat Mission In Vietnam." they stayed out overnight and then went back in to camp. Some mission. We covered their ass on the opposite shore while they got the glory. I still say that C 1/1 ran the "Last Mission" even though they did their 2 day photo-op non-mission.

After F Troop took the film crew back to safety, we cleared out our excess ammo, rather than turn it back in. We wrapped our main bun rounds together and tossed them into the river and blew them, along with hand grenades, C-4, M-79 rounds, etc. etc. The villagers hearing the noise, rushed out to dive in the river to retrieve the stunned fish. We also shot off most the M-60, 50 cal, M-79, and M-16 rounds; all but a magazine or so and a belt or two.

The next morning we were to head back in to base camp; it was decided that after 46 days of driving point (without tripping any mines) I wouldn't be leading the troop back in the front gates, past the waiting UPI cameras. SSG Spivey, who I had a fight with months earlier that got me busted, would run point in his APC. Since he and his driver were so used to tracking behind the column, he drove out in the same tracks that I brought us in on. I hollered on the radio once that he was an idiot for running in my tracks. A few short minutes later I heard an explosion from up ahead in the column. They had hit a mine that was planted by the VC the night before,

Grant Coble

throwing a track and tossing the crew around a bit. Thankfully no one was hurt.

My headset then crackled with, "Hill, move up and run back and forth alongside Spivey's track to tramp down the brush so they can change tracks." Yeah, right! There we sat, like sitting ducks, with LOW to NO ammo, waiting for fat Spivey's crew to repair their track so we can get back to camp. The UPI crew did wait for him though, ridding high in his TC hatch, looking like a black Patton his self.

The next few days were spent thoroughly cleaning our tracks for turn-in to the ARVNS. What a kick-in-the-pants that was. We knew they would be captured by the NVA soon enough. The depot that we drove them afterwards was huge. Hueys still in crates stacked two high, Duece-and-a-halfs lined up like at a huge new car lot, an we were giving it all to the ARVNs who would loose it to the NVA.

All that was left to dispense with were us Troopers; the rule was, if you had more than 8 month in-country, you could go rotate home or to your next duty station, if you had less than 8 months you were reassigned in-country. I had 9 months, so I was going stateside to finish my 4 years re-up after being stationed in Germany.

The orders came down in alphabetical order. A, B, C, D, E, H, I......Hey, What The Hell??!! You forgot Hill! I, J, K, L all the way to Z. But still no Hill. I waited a day or two along with the Mess Sgt., Medical Team, First Sgt. and a couple of other admin guys that were closing up shop. I just wandered around base camp, digging in dumpsters for all kinds of supplies and goodies that I could play with. A case of Kabar knives I found became a great way to pass time using my hooch as a dartboard. I even got to where I could walk 10 paces and fire and hit the bulls-eye.

Anyway, my First Shirt eventually sent me down to Personnel to check on my orders. Oh, my records were missing, and they would cut new orders for me, "Where did I want to go?" "Fort Carson, Colorado," me thinks. "Done," says the clerk. All I had to do was go back to the former Camp Faulkner and wait another day and a wake-up for my orders an ride out.

At the repo-depo waiting to process out and catch our Freedom Bird, we heard that the NVA had started a major offensive push south. All I had was one of the Kabar knives that I tried to take home but had confiscated.

We loaded the Bird around 23:00 on 31 March, an sat on the runway waiting, for what, we didn't know. Was the Army going to pull us back off the plane an give us an M-16 to fight back the advancing hoards? Nah, we just sat there until 01:00 on 1 April, 1972, April Fools Day an the whole plane got paid $65.00 each combat pay for April. Our final FTA.

3/21/1972, Left 23 Infantry Division to rejoin 1st Armored Division, Schwabach,
Germany
Last radio transmission in Vietnam:
From: CDR, 1/1 Cavalry   1400 Hours
To: 197th IN BDE S-3   21 March, 1972

The 1st Regiment of Dragoons requests permission to leave your net.

Closing a chapter in Vietnam

After 56 months of continuous combat operations from Chu Lai to the DMZ accounting for more than 6000 confirmed enemy KIA, innumerable weapons and over 50 tons of rice captured, the 1st Squadron, 1st Cavalry ends its combat mission in the Republic of South Vietnam. The 1st Regiment of Dragoons, the most battle honored unit in the United States armed forces, after adding one Presidential Unit Citation, 2 Valorous Citations and 3 Vietnamese Crosses of Gallantry With Palm to its 80 Battle Streamers, re-deploys to its parent unit (1st Armored Division in Ansbach, Germany). This Squadron, which has participated in such operations as Tet-68, Tam Ky, Pineapple Forest, Craterville, Cigar Island, Burlington Trail, Que Son Valley, Cane Field, and Lan Son 719, closes its tactical operations center and radio net at this time. We leave the 196th Infantry Brigade now truly a Light Brigade. In parting, we leave our Blackhawk Motto for our comrades in arms: "Animo Et Fide - Courageous And Faithful"

C Troop, 1/1 Cavalry   Camp Pitman
APO 09142   Weiden, FRG 1200-1400, 1 December, 1978
Item No.   Time (In)
1   1200

The 1st Squadron, 1st Cavalry, 1st Regiment of Dragoons assumed the protection of the free world on this day. 1st SGT James E. Taylor assumed duties as the first operations NCO.

Logged JET

August 27, 2003, 11:00AM, Fort Knox, Kentucky, Veterans of Charlie Troop, 1st Squadron, 1st Regiment of Dragoons came together for the first time as a unit since the Vietnam War at Fort Knox, Kentucky. The 4 day event was concluded with the "Reading Of The Names" of all our fallen Brothers. Several family members of our fallen Brothers were present and read the names of their loved ones. This helped give closure to those families so long wanted and needed. A plaque was uncovered and dedicated to our Fallen Brothers by Pat Monaghan and family members. The final home would be Kokomo, Indiana and Fire Base Howard County.

For us, the survivors, great sorrow and sadness for we miss you, our fallen brothers. You are in and on our minds daily. Your laughter, pain, what you looked like, and how you died stays with us daily through out our lives.

Oh, how we remember. We watch our children grow into young adults with such great pride yet we feel sorrow knowing you would not. Our laughter at a good joke mask the pain of you not being here to share the moment with us. Our triumphs in life are celebrated by our families yet you are missing. The every day meals and conversation but you are silent. The passing of a mother or father, brother or sister, son or daughter, aunt or uncle, but your strength and support eludes us. Your tears of joy and sadness are no more my brother. Our moments of sorrow are ever greater as we grasp each other in a hug but yet can't touch you. Forgive me, my brother, that even for a day, or a moment, I can't share with you a moment of my life. God, but I miss you! If ever there was a hero, it be you. Your bravery far exceeded mine.

Rest in Peace, my brother. For while I survived Hell, I am now living it with out you. Does this truly make me a survivor?

Anthony John Newman, "Blame,"
I talk with veterans,
Of a war in the past,
Most of us at that age,
Never expected to last.

But who can account,
For those ancient eyes,
They come from seeing death,
And becoming war wise.

A full measure of gratitude,
We never saw,
Just labels of killers,
Crazed from that war.

Those that had sent us,
Bailed out one for all,
None of them wishing,
To be caught holding the ball.

Politicians caught stealing,
With bureaucratic stealth,
None of them caring,
Just dreaming of wealth.

Who will answer the Veteran's plea?
The moral majority says not me, not me.

Scott "Tex" Gideon, "The Stone,"
The stone's a foundation so stout and sturdy
Some are called precious, so proud and pretty
The stone's a pathway for travelers to tread
Monuments of stone watch over the dead
The mill stone grinds the grain for the miller
The stone cold stare in the eyes of a killer
Stones cast at strangers we feel we must hurt

Grant Coble

Some call it war, but it is blood thirst
Stone of black granite that some call the wall
With names of those who answered the call
Stone is a altar to pile bones upon
When the heart of the stone and men beat as one
The stone is a world, now wasted and gone.

Dragoons

About The Author

Grant Coble resides in Kalamazoo, Michigan with his wife Joann and cat Callie, and dog Babe. He has two sons, Justin and Adam. This is Grant's first book, which is a compilation of historical facts and real life anecdotes from War Torn Vietnam- 1967-1972. Grant was in the United States Army from September, 1969-1971 and served with the Charlie Troop- 1st of the 1st Armored Cavalry. He became a tank commander in 1970. Grant enjoys fishing, writing, and "surviving" Michigan winters. (ice fishing!)

Made in the USA
Middletown, DE
05 March 2016